Women in Business

Women in Business

SUCCEEDING AS
A MANAGER,
PROFESSIONAL, OR
ENTREPRENEUR

BY

RONYA KOZMETSKY

★

TexasMonthlyPress

Texas Monthly Press
P.O. Box 1569
Austin, Texas 78767

A   B   C   D   E   F   G   H

Library of Congress Cataloging-in-Publication Data

Kozmetsky, Ronya.
   Women in business / Ronya Kozmetsky.
     p.   cm.
   ISBN 0-87719-177-8
   1. Women executives—United States.   2. Women in business—
United States.   3. Self-employed women—United States.   I. Title.
HD6054.3.K68   1989
658'.0023'73—dc20   89-37616
                                               CIP

Book Design by David Timmons

Contents

Acknowledgments • **vii**
Preface • **ix**

PART ONE: NETWORKING WOMEN • **1**

One:
Our Beginning: *Who Else Is Out There?* • **5**

Two:
Networking Women: *Who Understands Me?* • **9**

Three:
Women as Leaders: *Who Am I?* • **15**

Four:
Making It: *Do I Want to Be a Leader?* • **25**

PART TWO: WOMEN IN GENERAL AREAS OF MANAGEMENT • **33**

Five:
Being a Good Boss: *How Can I Make a Difference?* • **35**

Six:
Aiming for the Top: *Who's on My Side?* • **51**

Seven:
Mixing Business with Family: *How Do I Relate?* • **63**

PART THREE: WOMEN IN ENTREPRENEURSHIP • 73

Eight:

The Entrepreneur: *Should I Be on My Own?* • 75

Nine:

Financing My Own Business: *Where Do I Turn?* • 85

Ten:

Dealing with Risks: *How Can I Protect Myself and Others?* • 101

Eleven:

Getting Started: *What Do I Do First?* • 115

Twelve:

Getting Started: *How Do I Make It Happen?* • 123

PART FOUR: WOMEN IN PERSPECTIVE • 135

Thirteen:

The Changing Role of American Women • 137

Acknowledgments

Writing this book has been possible because the members of Women in Management have shared their creative and innovative experiences with so much generosity and good humor. Through the book I hope to reciprocate their gift, making their wisdom available to other women. I serve as their communicator. It is my duty to share their thoughts so they may enjoy the satisfaction of knowing that their experiences have helped others; that through their open discussion and self-examination they have made it possible for women to learn from other women. I also want to thank Joanne St. John, who edited this manuscript. Without her ability to organize the thoughts and ideas so clearly, this book would not have happened. Most of all, I want to thank my husband not only for his wisdom and constructive suggestions but for his total support and constant encouragement to write this book.

Ronya Kozmetsky
Austin, Texas

Preface

This book is offered in the belief that there is — and should be — a difference between men and women in their styles of management. I don't mean to suggest that the management style that is characteristic of women is any better or any worse than that characteristic of men, just different. Women have had an opportunity to observe and assimilate some of the best management techniques developed and practiced by their male colleagues. Now some techniques developed and used successfully by women managers are included in this book. I hope that some of them may be helpful to managers of both sexes, and that some of the ideas expressed here will help both women and men to examine the differences in their management styles and to build positively on those differences.

Women are relatively new at the game of management and have much to learn — from men, certainly, but also from women. They can learn from female role models who now exist and, as I hope this book will demonstrate, they can also learn from women like themselves who are still in the midst of struggling, experiencing, trying, succeeding, sometimes failing, and trying again. The substance of this book is taken directly from several years of meetings of the Women in Management (WIM) group in Austin, Texas.

A chance remark by a woman who had inherited a growing

business when she was suddenly widowed led to the formation of the group. Her frustration at having "no one to *talk* to about my business who can understand my point of view" struck a responsive chord in several of us who had experienced a similar need. She was a woman brand-new to a computer-related business venture. At that time the field was dominated by men, and she literally had no women acquaintances with comparable experiences, worries, and problems who could understand, compare notes, and offer suggestions. Her sense of isolation and need mirrored what others of us had felt, and we decided to band together to offer one another an informal support structure.

The result has been a strong, viable group that has met for several years to pool experience, seek advice, and offer reinforcement. The remarks quoted in this book are reproduced from transcripts of some of our meetings. I hope our painfully gained knowledge, as reflected here, will help convey one of the most positive lessons women in management positions can learn: they aren't alone. Their problems, frustrations, and challenges are shared by thousands of other women, but each of these women has gained knowledge and experience that can be of value to others like her.

While the book is directed toward women, I hope it will also be of some value to men, especially those who work with and for us, and those who love us and offer us emotional support. In reading this book, men can learn a bit more about our fears and frustrations, our motivations, our objectives, and our triumphs. By understanding us better, they may find it easier to interact with us in the business and professional world. Because that is where they'll find us — in increasing numbers and in ever more significant roles. Open communication between men and women in their working lives, as well as their personal lives, can help to build a synergistic system that will be both intellectually stimulating and materially rewarding.

Today women are in management, both entrepreneurial and corporate, and we're here to stay. We want that fact to be a cause of celebration for both sexes.

PART ONE

NETWORKING WOMEN

A new phenomenon occurring today is what our group likes to call "womantime"; it is a time in which business and professional women are finally coming into their own, exploring and enjoying their growing leadership roles.

In womantime we are looking at new avenues for getting together and testing our emerging power. By exploring ways to communicate with like-minded career women, more and more of us are developing work-related interrelationships that seem natural for men. Women have discovered the gratifications of networking. The network has not been an easy concept for women to grasp or implement, but we are coming to appreciate its value. As women, however, we are enjoying the opportunity of putting our own stamp on the concept. As *we* define networking, it is the act of reaching out to other career women, sharing through informal group interaction what each of us knows best, asking questions, and offering advice. By describing our problems, challenges, and triumphs we help one another face and deal more effectively with similar situations, and, most importantly, each of us gains security in knowing she is not alone. There is real reinforcement in knowing that ideas we offer are actually admired and implemented by other women, that the hard-won wisdom that we may dismiss in ourselves is considered by others to be not just worthwhile, but downright terrific!

Men have informal means of networking: business lunches, athletic clubs, golf, after-work drinks and conversation. Many women lack that casual reinforcement from peers. A women's group represents a deliberate effort to create an environment that most men take for granted. A network is a platform for airing our ideas and our miseries. We can discuss our successes, our failures, and our insecurities without fear of ridicule or misunderstanding. We can learn from others, and we can also share our own experience. Through pooling our experience and insights, we *all* learn to be better, more humane managers.

We are using networking techniques to serve our own particular needs. Networking can help us all to grow in our recognition, understanding, and appreciation of what we know and what we do well. It can help us accelerate our career advancement. It may be especially helpful for those of us who are in a hurry, who don't want to wait to achieve our places at the top, and who don't mind taking a risk to get there quickly. A whole new career dimension has opened up for us in achieving our objectives. This is the exciting and developing role of women entrepreneurs. Between 1974 and 1984, the number of self-employed women grew 74 percent, or six times faster than the number of self-employed men.[1]

Many women who are established in upwardly mobile careers, especially those who are entrepreneurially inclined, do not have the time or resources to pursue further education through traditional avenues, such as returning to school for advanced degrees or undertaking active programs of self-learning and research. Instead, many of these women have discovered that networking — tapping the enormous wealth of experience and organizational talents represented by a group of ambitious, innovative career women — can allow them a kind of time compression. Such networks can enable women to leapfrog toward career goals instead of playing catch-up. Through networks women can broaden their horizons, refine their own concepts of good management techniques, and reinforce their sense of self-worth. This can be an especially heady experience in a group where everyone is a "chief," and there are no "Indians."

---

[1]Robert D. Hisrich, *Entrepreneurship, Intrapreneurship, and Venture Capital: The Foundations of Economic Renaissance.* (Lexington, Mass., and Toronto, Canada: D.C. Heath & Co., 1986)

Our Beginning

Who Else Is Out There?

As recently as five years ago, we women who were in business and management positions in Austin, Texas, were pretty much on our own. Each of us felt there was really no one to share her perspective. Male mentors most often couldn't comprehend our special frustrations. The woman next door was usually in a totally different life situation and had no way to relate or understand. And for most of us there wasn't enough time in the day to accomplish essentials, let alone to look around for others who might share our situation and our needs.

I had an opportunity to speak at a University of Texas panel on management development for women executives, and I was overwhelmed at the response. It was astonishing how many women came forward to thank me for expressing their own feelings, and for letting them know they weren't alone. After that response, I decided something really should be done for these women. I called a few women I knew, and each one invited a few other women who were in leadership positions in business or in their professions. Ten of us got together for lunch and gave birth to an exciting idea. A whole new organization was designed on the restaurant's paper napkins during our meal. As we voiced our collective frustrations we realized that we had an urgent need, and together we conceived a format to meet that need. We would call our group "Women in Management." Since we all *were* in management, we wouldn't need a formal organizational structure: no officers, no bylaws, and no "Robert's Rules." The group's only purpose would be to offer support and networking, helping each other by sharing our unique and priceless experience. We would record our meetings so that women attending could take away for future reference a tangible reminder of the collective business and personal wisdom evoked during the course of each meeting.

Our group offered participants an opportunity to open up to many other women who also felt penalized by career pressures that made them miss important milestones as their children grew up; to share the bewilderment and embarrassment of applying for a bank loan for the first time; and to seek informal and supportive advice about how to locate and choose a good accountant, attorney, and other professional advisors.

A surprise bonus we all realized was that when the group started talking together we revealed an amazing array of "street smarts." Collectively we represented an invaluable resource. We had a wealth of practical information that couldn't be obtained from textbooks or classes. We knew and could advise one another about problems and challenges facing women managers because among us we'd faced — and survived — most of them.

Our group has been an incredibly fluid and dynamic collection of women. Women stay away for weeks and months as their careers take them in new directions. They come back to touch base, or when they have a particular problem and feel the need for support from peers. The dynamics change over time as new women come in and present their needs and their special skills and knowledge. The group is never stagnant because with new participants and new experiences, we are constantly exposed to new ideas and challenges. Our range of professions and businesses is great, as is the range of ages and experience. Some of us are entrepreneurs, some executives in corporations, some established professionals; some are just starting out in a professional practice or taking the first steps up the corporate ladder, while others are wondering about the wisdom of starting a new business. The areas of expertise represented by the greatest number of women are accounting, marketing, public relations, the law, and many areas of entrepreneurship. We have representatives of Fortune 500 companies and of one-woman businesses. We have women from real estate and development, research organizations, the nonprofit sector, education, retail, private investment, financial planning, the banking industry, the government, health care, print and nonprint media, the computer hardware and software industries, psychology, architecture, the building industry, manufacturing, the clothing industry, public service organizations, the culinary industry, and an array of consulting practices.

Our ages cover almost as wide a span as do our fields of endeavor. We have women starting their first careers, some of them in their twenties and some of them grandmothers. Some of our women are at the peak of their professional achievement after being in the work force for two decades or more, others are just beginning to face the choices that confront women as they juggle career ambitions with ambitions for marriage and a family.

What we all have in common is our enthusiasm for work, our drive to achieve, and our recognition that we have few, if any, female role models in the areas we have chosen for ourselves. We feel both awed and humbled that we are groundbreakers for women who will follow us, and we do not take this responsibility lightly.

We have all benefited from our group, from the wisdom others have shared with us, and from the gratification of having knowledge and experience that is valuable to our peers. Now we hope that other women can also benefit from our experience.

With this book, we seek to share the strengths and the insights that have grown out of our Women in Management network. For all of us, the experience of working with this small group of outstanding women has instilled confidence that women, especially those in management and other leadership positions, will make an important contribution to bettering the world, particularly for our children and the society they will inherit.

Networking Women

Who Understands Me?

WHO ARE MY PEERS?

It's one thing for us women to believe our time has come, it's quite another to start acting that way. To achieve our potential, we all need reinforcement. One way to find out who we are and what we can do is by regular, informal interaction with other career women who have similar needs and circumstances. Our Women in Management group has afforded its participants the nurturing and encouragement, as well as the hard information, necessary to our growth as business and professional leaders.

When we started the group several years ago we recognized that female role models were very scarce in the areas we had chosen for ourselves. While there have always been a few women prominent in the professions and in business, women in management and women entrepreneurs in particular are a relatively recent phenomenon. Only in the last 10 years or so have women participated in these areas in appreciable numbers. Many of the women who have achieved leadership roles have come to them totally without preparation, almost falling into the world of management. For such women, lack of training for the management role has bred lack of confidence in how to be a good manager and a good boss. The only example many women have had is a negative one: possibly a male manager whose mistakes they don't want to repeat, or a female manager who strives to outdo her male colleagues at their own game.

Recognizing that a gap existed in our preparation for leadership, those of us in the Women in Management group saw an excellent opportunity to learn from one another, to get practical advice from those who had achieved some success as managers and entrepreneurs, and to share our collective concern as women in being better bosses, and better managers, than most of those we had seen and experienced. We felt we could not only learn from one another, but also could reinforce one another in becoming, and urging others to become, the kind of bosses who "care" about people, as well as the bottom line.

Seminar leaders often ask participants to list five persons whom they most admire. Rarely does someone list his or her boss. As a group, we've deplored that kind of negative impact — or absence of positive impact — that bosses have on their staff. One of our goals is to change negative images of management by becoming the kind of managers who *will* be admired and respected. Whether as managers or entrepreneurs, we want to become part of a new generation of "boss role models."

While most of us haven't had the luxury of learning to manage by observing others' examples and sharing their experiences, we *have* come into our leadership roles with certain undeniable advantages. One is that we face our future with almost an entire page of "white space." White space is a concept borrowed from journalism, advertising, and public relations. In advertising jargon, white space is the blank part of a page that has no copy or graphics.

The benefit we women have in our white space is an absence of bad management habits or obsolete leadership attitudes that have to be overcome. Without the intellectual baggage of a feminine business tradition, we are unconstrained by preconceived notions of how to do things. We can start filling in our white space by adopting the best leadership models from achievers of either sex, and then by bringing in our own unique, creative, and positive leadership guidelines.

RESPONSIBILITY AND ACCOUNTABILITY

One of the most overwhelming aspects of our new leadership roles is facing the responsibility and accountability that are essential ingredients of leadership in business and professional life. While many women who assume major volunteer jobs take on enormous responsibility, they seldom experience the degree of accountability that is an essential ingredient of a management position. We've talked a lot about this in our group: most of us are properly sobered by the weight of the new powers and obligations we already have, and by the awareness that they will increase with time and greater success. We have grown sensitive to the full accountability that is the nature of the leadership role. We are trying to change the way we think, so that we can accelerate our progress as leaders and fill our new roles efficiently and effectively.

American society, and the world as a whole, both expect and demand that women accept personal responsibility for building a more civilized world. In our traditional roles as mothers, we women have assumed a social obligation to civilize and improve the world. As we are becoming aware of our emerging woman-power and society's growing and changing expectations of us, our WIM group in Austin, Texas, is trying to make a deep and conscious commitment to using that power wisely: a kind of "power of positive group thinking" approach. Surprisingly, most women still haven't perceived the extent of our power base. They haven't begun to appreciate what women can do if they support one another, organize, and work toward common goals. When the realization comes, its potential will be awesome. Then we must be aware of and attuned to the sensitive nature of real power and the potential for misusing it. We must take care not to abuse our newfound strength, but rather to direct its use toward the good of society.

An excellent example of how women can use their collective power for the good of society is the problem of child care. For many years child care was perceived as a "woman's issue," but with more than 50 percent of mothers employed outside the home the issue has taken on much larger dimensions. Recognition of child care as a community and social issue has occurred largely through the educational effort of women who have come together to create an effective political lobby. Right here in Austin the political importance of the issue is attested by the creation of the City of Austin Commission on Child Care that is seeking advice from prominent women (some of them in our WIM group) in formulating policy. Both national political parties are now acknowledging the importance of child care as a matter of national concern.

The opportunity and the temptation to misuse power are increasingly available to women. Some of us have had the strangely unsettling experience of discovering that wealth — that being in a position to control or dispense money — conveys enormous power. This is a relatively new situation for women who have accumulated substantial personal wealth as they have "made it" through their entrepreneurial or management successes. Without some preparation, or an unusually strong dose of common sense, such women are in grave danger of misinterpreting their own leadership capabilities and of abusing the power that their status has given them. One of our WIM members says, "I must always be on guard, and questioning why people treat me with special courtesy or deference. I must ask myself, 'Are they being nice to me because they really like me and believe in what I'm doing or because they know I control the distribution of large sums of money?' This makes me doubly cautious that I don't *abuse* this power as part of my own ego trip. Power is very heady stuff and those who are fortunate enough to have it must be constantly alert to the potential for its abuse."

Preparing women to understand and use power is an important task. Leadership Texas on the state level and Leadership America on a nationwide basis are two organizations that are striving to give women with leadership potential a real grounding in the meaning of power and how to use it wisely. These organizations prepare women for success and all the trappings that accompany it. Leadership Texas, which was established in 1974, is a program of the nonprofit Foundation for Women's Resources that "identifies and develops the finest women leaders in Texas. This program combines continuing education in leadership development, information and discussion of the major policy issues in Texas, and exposure to the philosophies and thoughts of the state's business, cultural, educational and political leaders." Such groups can do a great deal toward combating the temptations of sudden access to power.

BUILDING A NETWORK

Despite our keen interest in sharing experiences and striving together to be the best possible managers for our companies and for ourselves as human beings, we still came initially to our Women in Management group with some wariness — we were curious, a little reluctant to commit more of our precious time, but willing to try to start something new and potentially useful for other women like us. Those of us who have been in from the beginning feel especially proud of ourselves for taking the initiative in launching what has come to be an important part of our lives. New members have come in, some members have moved away, and some only attend occasionally. Members who are having a particular problem or facing a special crisis tend to be regulars; they come because they need the support the group can give. Although our membership is extremely fluid, we all consider ourselves a part of something very special and creative. All of us feel inspired by the openness, the trust, and the unqualified support that we gain from our associates in the group. Each of us has learned a tremendous amount, and each member has contributed greatly to what the others have learned. To our knowledge, WIM is unique in applying no restrictions on membership. Any woman who feels a need for this particular kind of group is welcome to participate and to share her experience. The only qualification for membership is interest.

For most of us, a regular support system is a novel experience. Women in American culture are not reared with the expectation of using, and becoming part of, a support system. Because of our inexperience with networking, at least in our business and professional lives, this informal association of Women in Management has been an exciting learning situation for most of us. Most who have participated, whether regularly or sporadically, have found the networking experience enormously satisfying.

Our informal, unstructured group has no leader. We agree

on a topic for our next session, or several sessions, and one or two of us volunteer to act as discussion leaders, doing some research and gathering materials that may enrich the understanding of our own experiences. We meet in the evening and we talk. Everyone participates, and most of us feel comfortable and unthreatened asking questions, sharing experiences, or offering advice. We look on ourselves as equals, with different strengths and weaknesses.

Our openness is possible because we all honor the confidentiality of the group. In keeping with that commitment to privacy, in the following chapters I shall address some of the questions each of us has asked herself, and that we've asked one another. I shall not name individuals or disclose information of a personal nature. I'll simply share ideas and experiences that have come from our group, ones we hope can be helpful to all of us as women in management or other leadership roles. As a case in point, one of our members recently suffered the agonies of starting a business, failing, and declaring bankruptcy. She very generously shared with us the details of her devastating experience, pointing out some decisions that hindsight showed to be serious errors. By openly discussing the painful steps leading to her own business failure, she hoped to help other entrepreneurs in the group avoid her mistakes. She would be embarrassed to have her identity revealed in this book but is willing to share with readers the knowledge gained from her own experience, knowing that personal confidentiality has been respected here.

THREE

Women as Leaders

Who Am I?

HOW DO I SEE MYSELF?
One of the first things we recognized in our Women in Management group was that many of us don't *see* ourselves as business or professional leaders. It seems that women in managerial or supervisory positions don't automatically consider themselves leaders. They are more inclined to think of women leaders in terms of Margaret Thatcher, the late Indira Gandhi, or Nobel Laureate Rosalyn Yalow—a select group of women who have earned notoriety through their singular achievements.

In our Women in Management group, the interpretation of leadership is far broader. We have begun to recognize that anyone who influences the behavior of others in a group is a potential leader. A good example of such leadership is the change in awareness of child care as a social issue, which was mentioned in the preceding chapter. Here in Austin, the efforts of a few very vocal women have had an enormous impact. The attention of social and business institutions in our community has been focused on this issue; and, through the City of Austin Commission for Child Care, steps are being taken to alleviate what is now recognized as a major problem in our society and *not* just the personal problem of working mothers. The women who have been responsible for this new awareness are leaders in every sense of the word.

Sometimes the groups and issues influenced by a leader are large, sometimes small, and they may exist in any institution within our society. A woman who is a volunteer running a large social agency or a fundraising drive needs all the qualifications and attributes of leadership, just as does the woman running a large company. Some of the women in our group actually have progressed to high-paying positions in the corporate world or in government agencies on the strength of what they've learned and accomplished in their volunteer experiences. It was a pleasant revelation to these women that some value was placed on their projects, which they had modestly considered "just volunteer work."

This tendency to minimize the significance of our roles is typical of women. Once we asked all the entrepreneurs in the group to raise their hands — and almost no one did, despite the fact that more than half of us present had started, or owned, our own companies. We just didn't see ourselves fitting the mold of "big-time entrepreneurs."

Sometimes it seems we really don't see ourselves as authority figures; sometimes we are unconsciously dishonest with ourselves, refusing to acknowledge how much authority we have assumed or been given; sometimes we are just plain afraid to face up to the fact that *we* are among the pioneers whom future generations of women will follow. As women we are just beginning to liberate ourselves from a cultural handicap: fear of success. Young women today are finally beginning to point with pride to their successes, no longer feeling compelled to disguise their achievements for fear their abilities will somehow become a cause for rejection. This is a heartening development and one that we women must encourage in one another by rejoicing in the accomplishments of our peers. Helping one another learn to enjoy our own successes and to applaud the successes of other women, rather than perceiving their success as a potential threat, is one of the most rewarding outcomes of our WIM group.

Absence of role models
We decided that one reason for our difficulty in perceiving our-

selves as leaders might be the absence in our own careers of role models whom we could emulate. There just haven't been a lot of women leaders in innovative business management against whom we can measure our own achievements. We may have problems seeing how far we've come, but we can always recognize some of our shortcomings! The lack of role models to serve as touchstones for our own success has a peculiar side effect: we learn more quickly from our failures than we do from our successes. We are sensitive to our failures (and there is always someone around to help us be aware of them), but we don't always recognize and go forward from our successes. We continue to dwell on the failures — what we feel we *don't* know or *haven't* experienced, or when we feel our knowledge or experience is *too limited* — but we seldom pay the same amount of attention to our triumphs. As we're able to measure ourselves more realistically in terms of other women who have made it, and to take pleasure in our own achievements, this tendency to minimize ourselves and our accomplishments will change. We'll begin to appreciate the relevance and value of what we know and have done, and we will see that there is virtually no limit to what we can do when given the motivation and desire to succeed.

Over and over again we have demonstrated at WIM the effectiveness of reinforcement by a peer group in helping women to gain the self-confidence necessary to take risks and to succeed. One of our members was the director of a social agency in Austin. Although she enjoyed her work, she felt unfulfilled, and she longed for the challenge of her own business. Those of us who had come to know and appreciate her talents urged her to strike out on her own — to realize her potential. She had saved a little money, and with our strong encouragement she left her secure position and launched her own company, offering training seminars. She has been very successful in her initial offerings, and is now expanding her programs and developing behavioral workshops for corporations. Her reputation is growing along with her business. The abilities existed all along; what this woman needed was the reinforcement and encouragement of people she respected, those who were able to understand and empathize with her goals and her fears.

During the years of WIM's existence, those of us who have achieved a modicum of success have shared with the group what we perceive to be the factors underlying our achievements, hoping that our personal "success mix" might help others who are still struggling. One of the young women in our group, who has built her own successful marketing and public relations firm, has organized several of her peers to act as mentors to a group of high school girls who need guidance and positive role models. At her instigation, some WIM members have acted as advisors to the young women — answering questions, listening to frustrations, and helping to spark ideas or suggest avenues that will help the younger women mold their futures.

Nevertheless, even recognizing that we have something to share that can be helpful to others, many of us still have a hard time being "the boss." When we talk about hiring and firing and personnel management, we find ourselves saying things like "I have this problem with authority. I have always viewed my bosses in a certain perspective. I don't want to be the authority figure for my employees." One of our members told us that when she took over the family business she was so reluctant to let people know she was in charge that she worked for two years as the company receptionist before openly assuming her role as president. Today this woman is very much in control of her software company, and under her leadership the business is prospering.

If we don't yet see ourselves as leaders, we at least agree on the kind of leadership we want to represent: the type of boss who *earns* the respect of her subordinates rather than *demands* it. While it might be possible for short periods of time to gain respect through superior technical skills, severity, or even inspired fear, these characteristics alone are not adequate to sustain it. We all feel strongly the importance of earning and keeping respect as leaders by being better human beings, by feeling and showing genuine concern for subordinates, and by giving them proper credit when they deserve it. This process is the hardest, the most frustrating, but also the most rewarding route to lasting respect from subordinates. The leader who achieves and sustains this kind of moral and ethical success gains enormous stature, and from this pinnacle seems to take off, with one success leading to another. An example here in Texas is Ann Richards, who started her political career as a county commissioner, went on to become State Treasurer of Texas, and has now achieved national prominence in the Democratic party. Throughout her career, Richards's style has been one of personal honor. She has built her success on her own abilities, not by preying on the weaknesses or foibles of her opponents. She has earned the respect and admiration of those who have worked for and with her, as well as those who have supported her campaigns. Her explosion onto the national political scene is a good example of *earned* success breeding even greater success.

Learning to sell ourselves

It seems significant to us that while many of us in the group are in professional or executive positions, at first we had to remind one another to bring and distribute business cards or brochures about our products or services. We didn't try to sell ourselves to one another, even though many of us were in businesses or professions that were of interest and value to the others. It wasn't that we were reluctant to discuss business. Rather, we simply weren't in the habit of talking business as a routine part of social communication. It was an exciting event at one of our meetings when one member (who happened to be an entrepreneur who had started her own software consulting firm) announced that she had made a big breakthrough: not only did she now carry business cards in her purse, but she also remembered to hand them out at appropriate moments. Because selling ourselves is not second nature for women, this was a real achievement! On the other hand, it almost seems like a reflex for men to whip out their business cards at the slightest opportunity.

It has become evident that we differ significantly from men in many areas.

- We don't automatically see ourselves — and we don't expect others to see us — as business leaders, managers, and entrepreneurs.

- We aren't in the habit of assuming, or persuading others, that we are prime candidates for bank or government loans or private investments.

- Many of us are not yet comfortable with the role we play in hiring, managing, leading, and sometimes losing or firing employees.

- We don't find it second nature to promote our businesses and services as something of likely interest to our acquaintances and friends.

We've come a long way, but we don't necessarily recognize or exploit that fact. We are, however, acutely aware of how far we still have to go in acknowledging, accepting, and using our own abilities.

Over the months, we have come to recognize that we can learn something from our male counterparts about how to view ourselves, how to deal with our leadership roles, how to let others know what we have to offer. We also recognize that we have an exciting opportunity: we have some valuable lessons to learn from men, but we also have a lot of important lessons of our own to teach. We *are* different, and, in many ways, we have a chance to be better just because we are women.

HOW DO I SEE WOMEN LEADERS?

While we don't necessarily see ourselves as leaders, we all have some pretty clear ideas about leadership characteristics in others. In particular, we've asked ourselves what qualities distinguish women leaders. The first characteristic we think women leaders need is self-confidence. It is a characteristic we recognize as vital to women in leadership, yet one most of us feel personally that we lack. To be a leader, then, a woman must strive to be self-confident. Interestingly, our emphasis on this characteristic corresponds to results reported by Christina Banks and her colleagues in a study of women participants in the Leadership Texas project.[2] Seventy-five percent of the women interviewed in this study identified self-confidence as the single most important trait for becoming a leader. As a leadership characteristic it was endorsed by 100 percent of the interviewees.

Another trait we attribute to leaders and top-level managers is readiness to assume responsibility for consequences of their own actions and those of their subordinates: "The buck stops here." As one member explained it, "You don't take the job if you aren't willing to accept responsibility — and blame — for whatever happens on that job."

Some of us think of leaders as agents of change — people who inspire others to work toward specific goals. We consider leaders to be very focused on goals, and believe they differ from other people in being more willing to take risks to achieve those goals. Leaders, "instead of waiting for an opportunity or a time that is right, *make* the opportunity. There's a sense of 'go for it baby; now is the time.' " We recognize that leaders have to guard against carrying these particular characteristics to negative extremes. The ability to motivate others can become simple manipulation; the capacity for focusing intently on specific goals and taking risks to achieve them can lead to insensitivity. Unfortunately, fairness does not enter into the leadership equation. Women must still be more capable and must work harder to achieve the same goals that many men take for granted. Even though it is slow, it is steady: we are making progress.

Sensitivity
The issue of sensitivity has been central to many of our discussions: being sensitive to the human condition requires constant awareness. Frequently in our monthly meetings the conversation will zero in on feelings. If one of us must make an unpopular decision affecting people in her organization, she is keenly aware of whose feelings are being stepped on, and she may carry her concern to the point of delaying the decision in order to make it as painless as possible for everyone involved. Still, we are equally aware of the negative impact of delaying a decision unduly. We're still trying to find the delicate balance that will combine the most positive results for people with the best management solutions. Management by gentle persuasion to change undesirable behavior is our ideal goal; despite difficulties and frustrations, we are convinced it is not unreachable. "I don't want to be the authority figure I've always resented," one of our women said. "I don't want to be a person who

says 'Do this. Do that.' I want people to work *with*, not *for*, me." By sharing our ideas and experiences, we hope to help one another achieve our goal of sensitive management by gentle persuasion, both for our own good and for the good of our companies.

One of our WIM members, a professional who heads a moderate-sized not-for-profit organization, shared with us her management techniques. Everyone who works in her organization is treated as a professional, and she expects each of them to perform as a professional. As a result, every one of the organization's employees is right there with the boss when crisis periods occur, putting forth whatever extra effort is required to achieve success. Nobody is concerned about status or position because everyone is responsible for getting the job done. From the "boss" down, they share in the demands and the rewards of achieving the organization's mission. There isn't a problem with the "this isn't in my job description" syndrome. Because the person in charge respects her staff and expects them to have the self-discipline necessary to achieve as professionals, they don't abuse her trust in them. Those who can't sustain the level of performance required generally leave to work in more structured and less demanding settings, but the turnover rate is very low.

We honestly believe that we can be instrumental in making such good management ideas work, and that we can help them spread for the benefit of society as a whole.

In considering leadership characteristics, we have been careful to note a virtually universal trait of leaders: they work hard. The long days, long weeks, and missed vacations go with the territory.

Having looked at a few of the characteristics common to women leaders, we can step back and take a new look at ourselves. Many of us exhibit precisely the characteristics we ascribe to leaders. Aren't we perceived by others as self-confident? Don't we take responsibility for our own actions and those of our subordinates? Aren't we agents of change in our own organizations and in our communities?

For those of us who are still fledgling executives, new in our professions, or just thinking about starting businesses, these discussions have led to new questions: *Have I got what it takes to be a leader?* and *Do I want to pay the price?*

---

[2]Christina O. Banks et al., "Motivations, Aspirations, Perceptions, Opinions, and Work Styles of Leadership Texas Women" (unpublished report, Department of Management, Graduate School of Business, The University of Texas at Austin, 1983).

FOUR

Making It

Do I Want to Be a Leader?

WHAT ARE MY MOTIVATIONS?

What motivates women who succeed in business, management, or professional careers? What inspires those who achieve high political office, or establish empires in real estate, investments, or the arts? What makes those women willing to put up with the pressures, the responsibility, and even the drudgery that comes with being the top banana? Why are they willing to take the heat? What are the forces driving them to do more than work at safe, comfortable, not very demanding careers that allow plenty of leisure time for family and other pleasurable activities?

As we look around in our group we ask one another: "Do we share those motivations? What are we striving to achieve? Do we *really* want to work this hard?"

What makes Sally run?

Of course, there is no single answer. One or two members swear it has "all been a series of accidents," or that "I've just been in the right place at the right time." Most of us recognize a more deliberate pattern. For some of us there is a constant striving for perfection — an inherent unwillingness to get by on the minimum that is necessary: "You get it done and you get it done right." There is a desire to leave nothing to chance:

"The details are what make you a success or failure. Everybody is full of big ideas. Very few people can actually pull together the effort, money, time, and energy necessary to accomplish a detailed task." "It's impossible to give the responsibility to somebody else, because they wouldn't have the drive." "If you're going to take the responsibility of management, particularly if you are running your own business, you often have to do things you don't want to do." "You feel directly responsible for what is happening."

For some women the motivation to achieve a leadership role is internal gratification: "If you are committed to making a success of something you have created, you are going to get inner satisfaction." "I could never give it up. I'd never go back and get myself employed again." For some, there's no option: "When your back is to the wall and you have no choice, it doesn't become a problem. It becomes a solution." "There's no decision; you are there." And for some there's pure joy in doing it: "This is great! I love it!" "Work was and is a passion for me. I love the process." "You don't start as an executive, you work your way up. You do the best job you can every single day, and the next step in your career grows out of it. Success is the icing on the cake." "It is not a question of power: I really love this challenge."

There's another motivator that most women hesitate to mention: *money.* Surveys have reported that women, when asked what they perceive to be their chief motivators in seeking self-employment, respond that they see in themselves the desire to be independent, to make a statement, to get greater job satisfaction, and to gain a sense of achievement. A desire to make money usually ranks no higher than the fourth or fifth motivator mentioned. Women in our group challenge these responses. We suggest that for most women who are willing to work hard enough to succeed in a leadership position, especially those who become entrepreneurs, the *principal* motivator, at least initially, is money. Women may perceive (or want to believe) that they are motivated by some higher-minded factors than "just" making money. But when they probe deeply and honestly, they will almost always acknowledge to themselves that money is their most powerful motivator. For all practical purposes, unless they make money, the other rewards of entrepreneurship just don't happen.

Many of the superachieving, high-energy women in our group are either single or divorced. Some are the sole support of their children. Many discovered very quickly that to earn enough money to support themselves or their families they had to make it big in some career. Entrepreneurship is often the only avenue for earning money at the levels they consider necessary. Money means different things to different women: it can mean independence, dignity, a way to survive as a single parent, an avenue of escape from a bad marriage, or a means of demonstrating equality with a male colleague. In our society it is also the chief emblem of success. The desire for more money drives some women to achieve top management positions. It drives others out of the corporate world and into entrepreneurship, where they can escape the limitations and inequities often imposed on women in established companies. Once their decision is made and the business launched, most women entrepreneurs are delighted that they have taken the plunge. At that point, money for its own sake may become secondary to the work satisfaction and ego gratification they experience.

TALENT, DRIVE, AND CREATIVITY

To succeed takes more than initiative, sacrifice, and hard work. What are some of the qualities successful women bring to their careers? What do they have that's special?

There is one key ingredient that every successful woman must have: a strong instinct for survival. With this quality — a sense of "surviving no matter what" — comes endurance, the capability to hang on. These are almost primitive female strengths, and they are fully expressed in women who become leaders. In these women the survival instinct extends beyond themselves to those depending on them. Survival aptitude goes hand in hand with the degree of ambition necessary to be a successful leader. Entrepreneurial women, especially, must be imbued with the sense of survival. Without the capacity to survive and endure, ambition will not be fulfilled.

The success story of one WIM entrepreneur demonstrates

her strong survival instinct, and how it worked for her. She had quit college to marry and raise a family. For several years her husband pursued his professional career and she was a homemaker, and then the marriage began to deteriorate. About 10 years ago she was faced with the prospect of finding a job to help support herself and her two children. She had no career to fall back on and no real work experience, so she realized she wasn't a hot prospect as an employee. Instead she decided to look for an entrepreneurial situation she felt she could handle. Living in a university community, she was aware that students required an enormous amount of copying; if she could supply that service more cheaply than other copying centers, she thought she could be successful. She borrowed $3,000 from friends, rented a tiny office cubicle in a building near the university, and opened her doors for business. In the beginning she worked 12- to 14-hour days to provide faster service than her competitors. Students discovered that her prices were lower and her product was better than that of other copying centers. Soon she was able to hire her first employee at minimum wage, promising more money as their combined hard work made the business grow. Grow it did, and today the company operates in several Austin locations, as well as in three other Texas cities. The company continues to beat the competition by providing a product that is both better and cheaper. Looking back now on her scary beginning, our friend is convinced that she had no choice but to succeed. She was neither equipped nor willing to work for someone else, and she *had* to earn a living for herself and her children. Her instinct for survival was so strong that she would not allow herself to consider failure as an option: growth and success were the only possibilities she would consider. Her business survival was an extension of her very basic human survival instinct — a different manifestation of the gut-level response that makes people hang on to life in seemingly impossible situations.

To our surprise, we have discovered that some of our most positive qualities as women arise from negatives, as in the example of our friend who succeeded as an entrepreneur because she didn't have the skills to be an employee. On a less dramatic level, most of us lack the self-confidence that seems to come naturally to men. How do we compensate? We try harder. Making a presentation, or doing a new assignment, we don't have the self-assurance to wing it, so we prepare well: we do our homework, gather our facts, arm ourselves with every bit of information we can lay our hands on. We use preparedness as a security blanket. We're not totally sure of our own self-worth and the absolute correctness of our opinions, so we're flexible. We don't want to go down with the ship, so we don't let the ship go down; we'd much rather change directions when we see that our present course is heading toward disaster. We stand a better chance of surviving because we don't have the "macho" quality of total self-assurance. Most of us don't start out in management positions. We have to work our way through the ranks, and in doing so we learn how things work: how to deal with the staff people who make or break most projects, where to turn for help in getting a job done. Because we don't have the luxury of total self-satisfaction, we keep on striving. We, and our companies, benefit. I hope we never lose these "negative" qualities!

In our group we try to emphasize the positive outgrowths of our negative qualities, and to capitalize on them. We have also tried to bring into the group as much outside information as possible to complement our own knowledge and experience. One of our members shared what she'd learned as a participant in a seminar at which several factors were identified that contribute to success in business, and some that lead to failure. Four positive attributes mentioned were *ingenuity* (being inventive, and taking charge: if you don't have a screwdriver, look for a dime); *expressivity* (sensitivity to people and the ability to express your feelings); *mastery* (wanting to improve your skills and learn more about your work); and *work orientation* (liking what you do). Four negative characteristics were competitiveness, verbal aggression, submissiveness, and excessive motivation. It seemed to us that members of our own group, and women in general, should score pretty well on a success meter, given these criteria. Women might excel in the positive quality of expressivity, since we often demonstrate great sensitivity to other people and are typically open in communicating. We also gave ourselves high marks for ingenuity, for an overwhelming desire to know as much as possible about our work and a willingness to work to improve our skills and knowledge, and we certainly have a work orientation.

ENERGY AND EFFICIENCY

What other characteristics do successful women in general, and we in particular, bring to our careers? One of our women pointed out two qualities that many successful women have, but haven't valued greatly in themselves. These are a high level of energy and an almost unconscious efficiency in their motor activity. She contends that women with a lot of energy are especially efficient in using and coordinating their bodies, and she believes that such high-energy women learn at an early age to conserve their resources by using the minimum amount of physical motion necessary to achieve a task. She claims "they almost automatically coordinate both hands with both feet to get a job done. In essence, they systematize their physical movements. A simple example is the fairly mechanical activity of vacuuming. A high-energy woman who is pressed for time learns to get through this chore as quickly as possible. She uses one hand to move a chair, the other to vacuum, automatically replacing the chair while moving the vacuum to the next spot. This simple coordination both reduces energy output and saves time in achieving the desired result. Most of us aren't even aware of these 'conservationist' techniques we learned as young girls, but we unconsciously carry them over into our business and professional lives." Our friend calls this internalized approach to saving time and energy "automatic survival efficiency."

Successful women become more efficient through constant practice, always striving to save a minute or two, to improve their productivity, to conserve their energy. Why? So that they may add one more activity to an already busy day. Our society has named them "superwomen," but that is a misnomer. They are really just careful planners who have become extremely good at conserving their physical and mental energy in order to achieve to their fullest capacities. If such women do have a secret weapon for success, it's their constant striving toward time conservation.

Differences in accomplishment may be attributed to differences in energy level: high-energy women achieve, while low-energy women don't. Further scrutiny often reveals that this difference in energy is really a difference in efficiency. Conserving our physical resources allows us to use our energy productively. Similarly, high achievers have learned to save energy in their thought processes. One of our group described her participation in negotiation sessions with groups of men. Typically, she says, she reaches her decision in a third to half the time required by her male colleagues, simply because she cannot afford the luxury of a leisurely decision-making process. The time condensing is important for her, since the "extra" tasks she must accomplish in her day prevent her from taking the additional minutes or hours that men seem to have, or seem to be willing to spend, for negotiations and discussion. A woman professor in our group, who sits on several college committees, says she solves this frustrating problem by always volunteering to chair committee meetings. "I won't allow time to be wasted in trivial discussion. I always have a tight agenda and stick to it. The men on my committees invariably comment, 'Gosh, we sure got a lot done, and it didn't take all day.' It doesn't seem to occur to them why the meetings are so successful."

In addition to survival efficiency and time condensing, our women believe that there are several important "feminine" traits we should develop and exploit. One is personality: "Your personal style really does communicate to people. If you don't run your business in a fashion consistent with your style, why should people deal with you? You are perpetuating a fraud." Another is feelings: "It's okay to be emotional, it's okay to tell people that you love them. If you don't do that, why live? Why run a business?" "Communicate and listen and allow yourself to feel and be in touch with what you feel. You can't discount it." There is clarity of purpose: "Always keep focused on your goal." Honest pride: "If you aren't proud of what you're selling, this most genuine thing that you can deliver, then you don't have any business being out there." And integrity: "Trust your instincts. Never do anything that doesn't feel good in your stomach, because if you do, it will be dishonest, and it will never work out." "The dignity with which you achieve your ends is as important as the ends themselves."

We agree that an appreciation for style — and what it conveys to the world — is a characteristic of the most successful women leaders. What we mean by "style," here, is a sense of distinction, an aura that separates a woman from those around her, that makes her stand out in a group. One of our women says, "It's like sex appeal. It's hard to describe, but if someone has it, you know it right away. If you don't already have an identifiable style, it is important to make a conscious effort to develop one, to become 'somebody,' and not just part of the crowd."

PART TWO

WOMEN IN GENERAL AREAS OF MANAGEMENT

There are two approaches to evaluating the progress women have made in achieving leadership roles. Many of the women in our group perceive an absence of giant strides in that direction, and deplore the many inequities that remain. Essentially, they take the "half-empty glass" approach. They may be right.

Others feel, however, that some strides have been made, and that they should be acknowledged. We find it counterproductive to dwell on what has *not* been accomplished, and prefer to emphasize the positive achievements of women managers and entrepreneurs. We see the glass for women in leadership as "half full."

In such areas as business management and finance, the doors of opportunity for women have opened dramatically. Many new and exciting areas of science and technology have also become accessible to women. And today, women fill nearly a third of all management positions in the United States.[3]

Some of our women note that only about 3.5 percent of Fortune 1000 directorships are held by women, while others counter that almost half of the thousand largest companies in the United States have at least one woman director. In 1986 there were 395 women sitting on the biggest corporate boards in the United States. In 1976 only 13 percent of Fortune 1000 companies had even one female board member, while in 1986, 44 percent of Fortune 1000 companies had a female board member.[4]

More than half the women appointed to directorships in 1986 had previous board experience. Even more significantly, the women who are tapped for directorships today are no longer chosen exclusively from the ranks of relatives of the chairman of the board, or widows of major stockholders. They are now being sought because they are seasoned business and professional persons who can make positive contributions to their respective corporations.[5]

[3]Regina E. Herzlinger, "Dancing on the Glass Ceiling," *Wall Street Journal* (February 17, 1988).

[4]*Savvy* (September 1987).

[5]Keith Bradsher, "Women Gain Numbers, Respect in Board Rooms," *Los Angeles Times* (March 17, 1988).

FIVE

Being a Good Boss

How Can I Make a Difference?

WHAT CAN I GIVE?

It's important for those of us who are entrepreneurs or top managers to acknowledge that we are, in fact, leaders. In today's society, a leader is a person who wields significant influence in his or her own corporation, in the community, in the state, or in the nation. Leaders are people who are in a position to affect the lives of others by changing attitudes and behavior in their organizations and their communities.

Because our numbers are still small, we women who achieve management positions have had leadership thrust upon us. So far, there aren't enough of us to go around. We're visible, and we automatically influence the lives of other women. When we achieve success in one area, we're assigned preeminence in other areas. And with our leadership roles come certain obligations. One is to make things different or better for other people. A part of our professional lives in which we can make a real contribution is in the supervision and training of those who report to us.

Whether we choose to become entrepreneurs or to make our careers in large corporations, in government, or in service agencies, most of us who become leaders also become bosses. In that role we have double responsibility: to use all of our special gifts as women (in addition to the skills we've learned as

businesspeople) to be the best and most nuturing managers
we possibly can be, and to be role models to the women who
will follow us (and possibly to some men who want to go beyond certain stereotypes we've been raised to expect).

That's a pretty tough assignment!

Networking and mentoring

We have two valuable tools at our disposal. One is networking.
As we come up through the ranks, we must begin to value and
maintain our contacts. Everyone we meet becomes a member
of our network. How actively we use and contribute to that
network will be one measure of our success in our own careers.
It will also measure how effective we are as role models. The
young people who work for us, and who follow us in building
their own careers, should expect to depend on, profit from,
and build on our networks. By reaching out we gain for ourselves and our subordinates new perspectives and new opportunities, and we are then able to offer new perspectives and
new opportunities to others.

Another tool is mentoring. In this area, both biologically
and culturally, women have an enormous advantage. We are
by instinct and by training the nurturers and educators of the
generation that follows us. Historically, women who have
sought employment outside the home have worked as nurses,
teachers, or in other situations where their capacity to care for
others has been a principal attribute. What could be more
natural than to extend that inclination and gift to those who
fall under our supervision during our careers? Our male counterparts are culturally disposed to see the next generation, or
the bright young star, as competitors. Why shouldn't we follow
our natural bent and view them as potential beneficiaries of all
we've learned and experienced? Their abilities can enhance
ours. They can enrich our ventures. If we cooperate and teach,
instead of competing and suppressing, don't we all benefit? By
embracing and helping our prospective successors, rather than
competing with and threatening them, we can help them grow
and develop. Their ultimate successes and contributions will
be a reflection of our own. And by encouraging their creativity
and innovation we too can learn, grow, and prosper.

One of our women described an unusual situation she experienced on joining a new company here in Austin, one in which women were heavily represented on the management team. "I feel that I have gained self-confidence in a personal area. I have been somewhat successful in most of the things I've tried to accomplish in business. But this company has really been interested in people as people — pushing us to better ourselves in our personal lives with more education if we want it — and just with everyday things, encouraging us to push ourselves on a personal level. That has been really nice and really new for me. Normally in business you walk in the door and you are pushed to get things done because of *their* needs. They do not consider whether *you* want something more for yourself."

Even in the recent past, the number of women in high leadership positions was quite small. In business management women were particularly scarce, and those few who made it up the ladder tended to seek mentors among their male colleagues. Today the ranks of women in management are growing, and so are the opportunities for these women leaders to serve as mentors for younger colleagues of both sexes.

One young member of WIM is striving to expand her business in the child care industry. She has chosen one of our older and better established members as her mentor, and periodically calls on the older woman for an hour or two of conversation. Occasionally the older woman makes a suggestion, offers some advice, or refers her to an information or service source, but most of the time she simply listens as the young woman struggles out loud to understand and resolve her problems. By acting as a sounding board and raising questions she provides an enormous amount of support to her young colleague. The act of articulating the situation to a more experienced listener helps the younger woman generate a host of alternatives, and a chance word may be enough to trigger a solution to what had seemed an overwhelming problem. For the older woman, this kind of interchange is often very rewarding. Being able to serve is gratifying, and so is the sense of intellectual growth and stimulation that comes from associating with an intelligent and able young person. She says, "It keeps my batteries recharged. I don't have a chance to stagnate or feel unproductive."

Relating to subordinates

We want to do an outstanding job as bosses. We don't want to fall into the familiar trap of using authority or power to substitute for leadership. We don't want to let self-importance substitute for self-awareness, or dictatorship for leadership. We want to influence and, when necessary, change behavior by example and by "gentle persuasion." Management by gentle persuasion is basically a marketing tool: it's a technique for making decisions that others want to follow. A manager who sells his or her idea or philosophy to staff members so successfully that it becomes "their" idea has learned the technique. Once a staff embraces an idea as their own and it works, they will sell it in turn to their own subordinates. This kind of management doesn't leave room for ego problems. The manager is concerned about his or her idea or philosophy being accepted, not about who gets credit for it. If the plan is successful, credit will spread in a ripple effect, and everyone will benefit.

We want to make management an art, not a craft. One woman in our group used two teachers to illustrate this distinction. One, the craftsman, has an adequate knowledge of the subject matter, puts in the necessary time doing preparation and working with students, and the students learn the material required of them. The second teacher is an artist, bringing to the classroom not only the subject knowledge and the willingness to work, but also the gift of inspiration. This teacher brings out in the students all their enthusiasm, creativity, and joy. They leave the classroom not only with an understanding of the subject matter, but also with a love for it and for learning.

As bosses we want to achieve the level of art: to inspire others to express their creative potential — and to reward them for it. In becoming conscious that we are role models in management, and therefore in leadership, we should always be aware of the impact we have on others. We should strive to use our status responsibly, and to exert a positive influence on our subordinates, our organizations, and our communities through our attitudes and our actions.

We've spent a lot of time discussing "management by gentle persuasion." The concept is borrowed from the American Quakers, who are truly gentle people. They do not believe in confrontation, or in resorting to an adversary position. Adopting their philosophy as bosses, we have many opportunities to use gentle persuasion in working with and motivating subordinates; for example, by encouraging them to explore their creative talents, offering help only if it is wanted and never forcing it, and by committing support and available resources to promoting and nurturing their ideas and suggestions. A woman in WIM who manages a software company tells us, "While they are in my organization, people will be treated with respect, as professionals. Being rude and not treating someone as a professional, regardless of his or her position, is a basis for being fired at my company."

In addition to sensitivity, another essential ingredient of this style of management is timing. A boss must be closely attuned to his or her people, and must have the intuitive sense of *when* a subordinate needs help, needs encouragement, or is ready to accept a challenge and release some creative energy. There's no point in opening the door to opportunity before the subordinate is ready to step through it and become a star. Insensitivity, as reflected in the inability to recognize and seize the moment or, conversely, in a tendency to force a situation before the time is right, is an unfortunate characteristic of bad managers.

It is especially important to be attuned to employees and to have them on our side during times of crisis or failure. Naturally, these are among the most difficult times either to be understanding or to practice leadership skills, but it can be done, as we were shown by the woman boss of a technology company. The company had spent considerable time and effort on a proposal for a government contract that was crucial to the company's growth and development. Technical and management personnel worked extraordinarily hard on the proposal, only to see the contract go to another company. With morale low as a result of the disappointment, the boss decided not to expect people to return to business as usual, but rather to open the problem for general discussion. She called a "Monday morning quarterbacking" session for everyone involved in writing the proposal. There was no vindictiveness or finger pointing, just a brainstorming session to decide where mistakes were made and what could be done differently in future proposals. Everyone had an opportunity to get rid of the bad feelings of losing, and to start planning for the next time on an upbeat note.

Another boss, this one male, uses another gently persuasive approach when his company is in a situation where it's hard for his subordinates to accept a new idea. "Trust me just once," he says. "If it doesn't work, you won't be asked to do this again, but please trust me this once." He sticks to his word, but more often than not his idea does work, and the employees find it easier to go along the next time.

Perhaps the only absolute rule in management by gentle persuasion is for a boss never to ask an employee to do something the boss wouldn't do. Using a mundane but sometimes emotional example: if a secretary doesn't like to get coffee, we agreed the boss should get it herself and bring the secretary a cup, too — perhaps with a gently teasing comment that it isn't in anyone's job description, but since coffee obviously makes the office (if not the world) go round, *somebody* has to do it! Humor plays a very big part in management by gentle persuasion. A sense of humor is perhaps the most important quality in being a good boss, especially when a company is going through rough times. Humor is the ultimate tension breaker.

One of the closest — and most critical — relationships any boss can have is with his or her secretary. The secretary has a key role in the boss's success or failure. It's the secretary who can open (or close) vital communications linkages, and keep the boss either on top of things or completely out of touch. The secretary can be an invaluable ally or a dangerous enemy, and much of the relationship depends on the boss's attitude from the first day they work together. When the boss and the secretary both are women, the relationship is an especially delicate one. The boss must show sensitivity and respect and must be a humane and caring person if she wants to win the loyalty and support of her secretary. It is the boss who must take the initiative in establishing the relationship. Still, some of our women were quick to point out that even the best of bosses can sometimes have an inefficient, ineffective, uncaring, or disloyal secretary. If the boss has done all she can to make their relationship work and to encourage and stimulate productivity in her secretary, but a problem still exists, she should fire the secretary *immediately*.

During the past 10 years the explosion in the field of information technology has led to a redefinition of the secretarial profession. As sophisticated word and data processing equipment becomes more generally available, many managers are becoming both computer literate and more self-sufficient. Many of the tasks that were once the responsibility of the secretary are now assumed by the executive, and the former secretary can be freed to become more of an administrative assistant or an associate who can learn new technological skills to support her boss. Schools and colleges will have to restructure their curricula to prepare students at all levels to adapt to a changing office environment, and on-the-job retraining programs will become increasingly important to keep employees' skills relevant to the new situation. The boss who is willing to take full advantage of the information tools available will gain an important edge in decision making. The secretary who is liberated from many repetitious routine office jobs also gains an advantage in being able to learn new skills and assume more creative responsibility. Working out the new office relationships so that both the boss and the secretary perform to the best of their abilities—and find fulfillment in their changing roles—is a challenge of our new information environment.

The loyalty and dedication of employees is something every boss should strive for. In any new entrepreneurial venture it is absolutely imperative. The employees must have as much dedication to making the business succeed as does the entrepreneur. The entrepreneur must be prepared to give 100 percent plus, and so must the employees if the business is to succeed. Let's assume our entrepreneur is a woman, determined to make her new business go, who is aware that her employees are a key ingredient for success. She can win their support and commitment in several ways. First, she must demonstrate the extent of her own commitment by doing more than she asks anyone else to do. Then she must reward her employees' loyalty with praise and thanks. Finally, she should be aware of the families of her employees, and the sacrifices that they are making for her business. Some of our women have found it works wonderfully well to involve employees' families by going to them and explaining the situation. "Just say, 'I'm asking a great deal of your mother because she's a very important part of this business. Once we get over this hump, she'll have more time to be with you. And if I make it with this business, she'll make it too. There's a lot at stake for her, and I hope you'll put up with her schedule for a while.' " And, of course, when success *does* come, it's essential to share the rewards with the employees who've helped make it happen. Again, our women observed that when employees are not willing to give the kind of loyalty and dedication needed to get a new business off the ground, they should be fired. Everybody on the team must be committed, but the boss must be committed to an even greater extent.

To gain the respect and dedication of her employees, the new entrepreneur must show that their devotion and zeal will be rewarded through her all-out effort to achieve success for all of them. She must constantly demonstrate to her people that she is totally committed to the enterprise, the product, or the service. They must realize that her judgment, ability, and professional reputation are unquestionably centered on success. Leadership skills are most critical at the beginning stages of a business's growth, as one of our young WIM members is learning. She is struggling to get her technology-based company off the ground, and has brought several of her key employees with her to our meetings. Clearly, they are totally dedicated to the enterprise and to their boss. "I always work longer and harder than anyone else in the company," she told us. "I make every effort to prove to my employees that I know what I'm doing, and that the company will make it, through a combination of their efforts and abilities and my creativity and management."

PAYING OUR DEBTS
In fulfilling our roles as networkers, mentors, and "good boss-

es," we are really paying a debt. Although we may not be able to look back to entrepreneurial women as role models, we can certainly say thanks to the women who have preceded us and paid their dues as students, as professionals, and as business women by breaking away from the molds they were expected to fit. Their lot was harder than ours, and because they struggled against being confined by the conventional roles of women, we can move into entirely new areas with a minimum of resistance and at a far swifter pace.

Radicals have always been important in creating necessary change. Once change has occurred, communities need dedicated, responsible persons who will build and maintain solid institutions for the many who will follow. This has been just as true in the women's movement as in any other dramatic social or political movement. Only a little more than a decade ago, airlines wouldn't hire married women as flight attendants (then "stewardesses" or "hostesses"). A few women made themselves "deliberate victims" of the system by challenging this discriminatory regulation, and today cabin attendants of *both* sexes may be married or single, parents or childless: all have benefited. The radical women of the 1960s fought, and were ridiculed, fired, and even jailed for, issues that women in today's work force take totally for granted. We've not yet achieved total equality, but we have come an incredible distance thanks to these "deliberate victims" who knowingly placed themselves at risk to focus attention on social problems and to improve the lot of all women.

When we talk about deliberate victims, we refer to people who willingly put themselves in jeopardy to help initiate social changes that they feel are important. Martin Luther King, Jr., and his followers in the civil rights movement were deliberate victims in choosing civil disobedience as a means to achieve civil rights for the black people of this country. They knowingly defied authority and went to jail as a strategy to achieve their end. Deliberate victims, who know and choose a path of action that will have negative personal consequences, are quite different from innocent victims, who are simply in the wrong place at the wrong time and get swept up in circumstances that overwhelm them.

A recent example of women who have placed themselves in

the role of deliberate victims is a group of investors and banking professionals who recognized the unmet need of banking services for women equal to those available for men. One such group established a bank in a large city in competition with many existing financial institutions. Some of these women risked all their personal assets, some even borrowed money, in order to start a women's bank. The professionals who left secure positions in other banking establishments to go out on a limb with the women's bank also put themselves at risk. Regrettably the bank, First Woman's Bank of California, was not widely supported by the very women it was intended to help, which reflects an interesting fact about our society. We have been culturally conditioned to think of women as lacking the acumen to handle finances. Until the middle of the twentieth century there were still states that considered women their husbands' chattel; and if women did any banking or selling of property, it was allowed only when a man co-signed the legal documents.

This attitude of financial inferiority to men has been remarkably difficult to change — for women as well as for men. But gradually, the change is happening. One of the most important reasons behind the change was the passing of the Equal Credit Opportunity Act of 1974, which made it mandatory for a lending institution to take a woman's income into account when she applied for credit, without demanding her husband's approval or income status. The act prohibited discrimination on the basis of sex or marital status in the granting of credit. By allowing people to gain credit without respect to gender, this law opened the door to equal banking services for women.

Forward-looking institutions, such as the First Woman's Bank, had an essential role in making the transition a reality. In addition to making banking services available to women, even though women didn't flock to take advantage of them, First Woman's Bank performed a vital service in educating women to their new opportunities and to the support mechanisms available to them. In fact, the First Woman's Bank ceased operations when it was no longer needed — because other financial institutions had been receptive to the message the bank conveyed and had begun offering to women the services that were initially only available through the special banking institution. The bank, and the deliberate victims who were responsible for creating it, achieved the desired end. In this instance, the victims were successful not only in achieving their ends, but also in a financial sense: the bank was acquired by a larger financial institution (at a nice profit to the original women investors), and the new institution retained as president the woman who had served in that position for the women's bank.

It is the determination, courage, and selflessness of such women that we can repay by being superior managers, compassionate bosses, and outstanding role models.

GRACE UNDER PRESSURE: SETTING AN EXAMPLE

An area in which we can be very effective as bosses and role models is dealing with and resolving conflict. Logical, calm, and controlled behavior is extremely effective in defusing potentially explosive situations, whether they involve conflicts with colleagues or intervention and disciplinary action with subordinates. Women have a special opportunity in this area because of expectations that we will behave emotionally, if not downright irrationally, when faced with unpleasant or controversial situations.

Women in our group advise, "Let others lose their tempers. A woman's greatest strength is never to blow her cool." "No matter how provoking a situation becomes, being in control of your emotions at all times is a very powerful leadership strategy." Of course, to maintain such control takes enormous patience and concentration, but women in our group have learned that keeping their heads in negotiations or controversies where others may lose their tempers can create a distinct advantage for the cooler head. What makes this technique so effective, especially in situations where the other party is male, is that men in our culture tend to assume that women are emotionally unstable. A woman who demonstrates her ability to remain cool and logical under stress can be remarkably persuasive in putting across her ideas or opinions. By maintaining her composure and dignity, a woman not only can win arguments, but also can earn the respect of her peers and her subordinates. She can gain both prestige and a foothold on power by remaining firm and patient.

If adversaries, male or female, fall apart under stress, it's a perfect opportunity to "kill them with kindness." This is an incredibly effective technique because it's such an atypical approach to conflict. It immediately puts the adversary off balance, reducing his or her effectiveness. The capacity not to react or succumb to anger requires great patience and self-discipline. But developing the necessary patience will bring ample rewards. Maintaining control in a conflict situation can be a powerful management tool. In our society, failure to react is often perceived as weakness, yet the ability to show kindness and a calm response toward an angry colleague or subordinate actually takes great strength. Staying composed in the face of rage has an additional benefit. Anger temporarily clouds one's reasoning power. The angrier an adversary becomes, the less clear his or her thinking will be. The "cool" party in a conflict can often make points and gain valuable ground simply by thinking clearly and unemotionally. One way to achieve coolness is by learning to ignore. Few people understand the power of ignoring!

One of our WIM members owned a 10 percent share of an American Stock Exchange company and was also one of the company's directors. The company was in a period of crisis, and some very important policy decisions were being discussed at a board meeting. The woman found herself in total disagreement with another director. Our member was convinced that her policy was essential to the well-being of the company, while her counterpart was strongly opposed to it. The board quickly became polarized behind the positions taken by these two directors. The woman director had come to the meeting well prepared, since she had anticipated some resistance to her suggestion. Her adversary, on the other hand, was not prepared to have his position challenged, and he became louder and more insistent in defending his argument, even using ridicule and verbal abuse to try to shake the woman from her strongly advocated position. She stood her ground, never raising her voice or showing any anger. Being prepared, she was able to articulate logical arguments in favor of her recommendation, with facts to support those arguments. Her adversary became so frustrated in the course of the discussion that he lost all emotional control, letting his fury direct his actions. He stalked from the room without even trying a logical rebuttal of her position. Our member never lost her dignity, nor did she attempt to destroy the dignity of her adversary: he did that all by himself! Incidentally, the board supported the position advocated by our member, and over time the company's survival and recovery proved that hers had been the right policy. Being right, on top of being cool, gained her further respect from her fellow directors.

The lesson our member learned from this experience, which she shared with the WIM group, has served some of us very well as a management tool. That is: Control your own emotions, and ignore your adversary's outbursts. Our friend says, "I discovered I could be very calm, because I had done my homework ahead of time. I didn't waste any precious thinking time or energy on emotional flare-ups, or on resenting the insults my antagonist was hurling at me. They didn't hurt *me,* they made him look bad, and while he was shouting he couldn't either think straight or offer an intelligent argument. His emotional ranting was counterproductive, while my unemotional logic carried the day."

In addition to self-control and ignoring a lot, humor is another effective anger deflector. It also offers a way to deal with criticism or blame without losing dignity. It can neutralize an adversary's anger, and prevent further deterioration of a touchy situation. In using either humor or kindness against an angry person, whether colleague or subordinate, it is important to allow him or her a way out of the situation without losing face. Diminishing another person's dignity can create a long-term enmity that is harmful to both parties. It isn't always easy to hold one's ground and still leave an adversary a graceful "out" in a conflict situation, but this is a skill well worth developing.

Although it's a controversial concept, and repugnant to many liberated women, there can be real advantages to allowing others to look good at our expense, even to the point of occasionally "playing dumb" so that someone else may discover an answer toward which we're actually pointing. One of our women, who has a very successful political career, says she learned this lesson the hard way. "The short-term satisfaction of proving yourself 'the smartest kid on the block' loses its luster when you see your important and constructive proposals defeated by the opponents whose ignorance of the issues you've just exposed. I've found it far more productive to make myself the 'dummy,' asking leading questions that let my colleagues propose brilliant solutions to some of the problems we face. They get the credit and feel good about it, and the community benefits. It works well for all of us."

Taking the role of the dummy can also be very effective in a corporate setting, as some of our members observed. Take the example of a woman in our group who has, on more than one occasion, made an important contribution at a board meeting by asking the apparently "dumb" question others were embarrassed to ask. This willingness to expose herself sometimes saved face for others who had not done their homework, or who were simply afraid to show weakness by appearing ignorant or uninformed. Sometimes it allowed another director to take credit for a creative solution revealed by her question. And sometimes the right "dumb" question forced into the open important information that had been overlooked or was even deliberately suppressed, allowing the board to make an informed decision for the benefit of the corporation.

This technique of playing dumb is most effective when it is timed properly. Asking the dumb question at the right moment is the key. Obviously, playing dumb and asking questions at the right time is not the only function of any single director, and that role doesn't always fall to women directors. "Dumb" is used advisedly, since the person who plays that role is usually far from the perennial airhead. Rather, he or she is someone able to analyze the situation, think through the key question, and present it at precisely the right time to clarify the thinking of the entire board. It goes without saying that playing the role takes lots of advance preparation and the ability not only to present, but also to defend, a logical position on an important issue.

These techniques all have in common the suppression of ego: not having to have the last or loudest word, and being willing to allow others to look good at our expense. In developing the self-confidence to let others shine, we can help them develop even as we strengthen our own management skills.

SIX

Aiming for the Top

Who's on My Side?

WHERE IS MY SUPPORT GROUP?

One thing we recognized in forming our group was that women who get to the top, and those on their way, need a lot of emotional support. In addition to hard work, long hours, and the pressures of responsibility, personal trade-offs are required almost continually. To achieve the fairly long-range objectives of success, it's often necessary to defer ordinary gratifications that most people take for granted. To be an effective manager, it's frequently essential to make unpopular decisions and to perform unpleasant tasks. And along with progress up the ladder comes distance from former colleagues: information passed along the grapevine among peers is not readily passed upward to the boss.

Where do successful women get their support? How do they get reassurance that they're on the right track? Where do they get the emotional fortification to keep going? Groups like ours can certainly be one important source of reinforcement. Such groups are relatively new and, although still small in number, are growing rapidly in our cities. An interesting finding by Christina Banks and her colleagues in studying Leadership Texas women was that 78 percent of the women interviewed said their principal source of emotional support was themselves, and 66 percent said that they found themselves the best source of professional support as well. By far the next largest source of support, both emotional and professional, was from a spouse or significant other, but the percentages here were substantially lower than those for internal support (59 percent sought emotional support and 33 percent sought professional support from the spouse or significant other). This certainly bears out our impression that the most outstanding characteristic a woman leader needs is self-confidence! Women who succeed have had to learn to stand on their own feet both emotionally and professionally.

As women, our reliance on "gut instinct" has probably developed because we have had to provide our own internal support systems. We're always unconsciously developing our women's intuition out of a need for self-preservation and protection of our families. Successful women, in particular, must always be aware of protecting their flanks, consciously or unconsciously testing and developing the instinctual behavior that leads to personal and professional survival. There is a lot of "mother tiger" in most successful women.

Men are also threatened in the workplace, but not in the same way or to the same degree as successful women. As men and women begin to compete more equally, we shall probably see some of the sensitivities and protective mechanisms that are taken for granted by women being developed by men as well. If we're smart and careful, we women won't lose those survival-oriented qualities as men acquire them.

For women in business "survival," as we use it here, can be seen as the flip side of failure. A man who fails in business is often able to pull himself together, find a new money source, and start again — sometimes in as many as three or four different businesses before he succeeds. For a woman, failure takes on the dimensions of a terminal disease. Since women usually have very limited access to venture capital, and bank loans are still difficult for many women to obtain, a new woman entrepreneur's main source of funding is often money borrowed from family or friends. If her business gets in trouble or actually fails, going back to ask for more may not be an option. (A recent statistic from the Office of Economic Research at the Small Business Administration, quoted in the November 1985 issue of *Ms.* magazine, shows that women entrepreneurs, on the average, start their businesses with less than $10,000.) Therefore, the need to succeed at all costs to make her business survive is very real. A woman in business for herself must use all her energy and creative abilities to survive; she will generally sacrifice, work incredible hours, cut expenses to the bone, and endure untold privations just to cling to a chance at survival.

The position in which most new women entrepreneurs find themselves, starting their businesses with very modest borrowed capital, can be a positive force toward success of the business. A woman who has started her business with a small loan does not have the burden of a heavy debt service to support. This allows her to maintain a steady cash flow, which is really the life blood of a start-up venture. The ability to regulate cash flow, which is especially crucial in the first year of a new business, can greatly increase the potential staying power of the new entrepreneur. Another advantage to starting small is that the new entrepreneur can pace her growth. This means she can avoid the pitfall of getting caught up in too rapid growth, a phenomenon that kills off many new ventures.

The spouse and family as support

In our group, those of us who are married or have some stable relationship with another person, or those who have children at home, feel it is very important to have the understanding and backing of those people as we pursue our careers. Sometimes they don't share our interests and knowledge, but they certainly must accept our commitment if we are going to be comfortable in pursuing our goals. Often the support we're looking for is not purely emotional, but also practical: help in household chores, sharing of child rearing, and participation in social obligations. Some of us who are not married find that our careers allow us little time for an active social life outside professional contacts. Marriage and a family may be one more of the gratifications that we choose to defer, or it may be an option not pursued at all.

DELIBERATE CHOICES

Women embarking on a career today must face choices that were rarely considered even a generation ago. One of the most exciting results of the feminist movement has been the opening up of career opportunities for women. As the old stereotypes of "women's work" have been destroyed, and career options for women have become virtually limitless, there has also been some negative fallout. Some young women, faced with endless possibilities, find themselves paralyzed by the array of choices open to them. There are so many avenues to explore in the marketplace that making a career decision is more difficult than ever before. Ironically, when options were limited for a woman, there was far less personal frustration in making a choice and pursuing education or training for what she wanted to do when she "grew up." The last two decades represent a period of transition, and new frustrations, in "womantime." Some women have not yet learned how to manage their new freedom of choice, and many young women actually may see themselves at a disadvantage until greater experience with this newfound freedom of professional self-expression makes it less a constraint than an opportunity.

Sometimes the choice a career woman faces affects her personal relationships. One of our women summed it up this way: "You can put a lot of time and energy into a start-up company, and also build and grow a meaningful relationship, but it takes a lot of hard work. *Both* people really have to want the relationship and commit to it for it to survive." Another responded, "I think you have to recognize that you have a choice, and that you make the choice. You are better off to face the alternatives in that choice head-on. You have to realize that you have made a choice according to your priorities. I also believe that it hinges upon having a very supportive person as a partner in a relationship. My husband is extremely supportive and I could not have done without his support at that time. If he had not supported me, I would have faced the decision of leaving him or doing this other thing. I did not have to make that decision. I think that the worst situation you can get into if you are facing alternatives is not recognizing that there *are* alternatives and making a conscious choice. You must be aware that you might wake up sometime and regret having done it."

There are other life-altering choices that women must make today. When there is a real goal conflict, such as career versus marriage, as women we still have to make the hard choices to a far greater extent than do our male counterparts. In our society, men have been able to take marriage and a family for granted as an activity apart from their careers. Few women today have this luxury.

One example comes from an entrepreneur in our group whose husband was also an entrepreneur. Their careers were very separate, and both were very successful. For some time their scheduling presented no special problems. "I was working a great deal of the time. It didn't seem to bother my husband or my son. I felt a little guilty because I never cooked, but I solved this by hiring a housekeeper to come in every day and cook my son's dinner. My husband and I didn't eat much at night, so I didn't worry about us when a lot of times I would work at night. But then as the years went by and my husband became more successful, he hired people to help run his business and for the first time he had leisure to travel. He wanted me to go with him. Of course I couldn't, because I had to work. All of a sudden he was going off without me. I could see that my marriage was going to get in trouble if I wasn't careful, and I didn't want to sacrifice my marriage. It was a decision I had to make. I had to change my priorities." Her solution at that time was to sell her business and hold her marriage together. As it turned out, the marriage was later dissolved despite her decision.

Another example is a very successful corporate executive who has enthusiastically accepted each new career challenge and opportunity. She has advanced accordingly, and has been delighted with her progress. Suddenly, facing 40, she has recognized that she has effectively eliminated her opportunity for childbearing. She still loves her career, but she feels she has missed something important without consciously choosing to abandon that option.

Several other members of our group who have deferred plans for marriage and a family in order to pursue career goals find themselves bitter and frustrated. They know their biological clocks are running down, and sense that they have lost an important part of living. The bitterness comes because they believe they have never had equal options with their male colleagues. One of these women, who has worked single-mindedly to advance her career, is now approaching 40 and has decided she wants to marry and have children. The man with whom she has a long-standing relationship does not share this interest. He has been married and divorced, has two children, and has no intention of starting a family again.

What these women are experiencing is a growing social phenomenon. They, and most other contemporary women, want "to have it all, and at the same time." As yet, we can't propose a satisfactory solution. It is a problem that our society must address.

It's not only family life that may be sacrificed to a career. Friends, hobbies, travel, or further education may all be postponed in the name of immediate demands to succeed. Sometimes we make choices unintentionally, by postponing things that are important to us in favor of what our jobs demand "right now."

Whether we choose to remain single or to marry, to have a family or to remain childless, to take a trip abroad or to defer a vacation while completing an important project, we are all forced to establish priorities. Very, very few of us can do it all simultaneously. Many young women defer friendships, or travel, or marriage plans, or childbearing until they've established themselves on an upward path in their careers. For some the career demands continue to be so great, and so stimulating, that the temporary interruption in social life, or seeing the world, or establishing a family becomes permanent. For others there comes a time when the need for friends or for the enrichment of travel is acute, or when the desire to fulfill the nesting urge becomes overwhelming, but by then total dedication to career goals has limited their options.

Still other women who have tried to juggle a flourishing career, regular social contacts, and a marriage may find themselves abandoning — or abandoned by — either their occupations or their personal interests. This is not fair, but it *is* true. We are still forced to make trade-offs to a far greater extent than men. Whichever choice we make, it should be conscious and deliberate. It is important for us to know what we're giving up, and what we're getting in exchange. We must recognize that whatever we choose, there's always a price. Whatever the choice we make, we must feel comfortable that the results are worth the sacrifice. For many women this situation brings home the cliche, "There is no such thing as a free lunch."

Too many women have been innocent victims of the feminist movement because they weren't conscious of the implications of their early choices. They've embraced open relationships that didn't interfere with exciting career opportunities only to be trapped 10 or 15 years later by changing priorities. They failed to recognize at the outset that their liberated choices were shutting off options. This is an unpopular thought, but the women's movement has, in many ways, benefited men by extending their freedom from commitments at the expense of women. We must learn to make long-range plans that put *us* in charge of our priorities!

Our discussions in the WIM group often center on guidelines for establishing our priorities. We're still agonizing over the question; so far there are no easy solutions. The fact that we're aware of the problem and struggling with it leads us to hope that some day soon a bright, creative person will discover an answer and share it with us: a practical, forward-looking, long-range plan that will help women make the right decisions about their life priorities.

An overwhelming frustration for many upwardly mobile women is aborting their careers to stay at home while caring for small children, at least until they are of school age. Many such women feel penalized for taking the time to be mothers. Although they believe that staying at home with their children and watching them grow is too precious to miss, losing out on their careers is still a bitter pill. Few women consider how much their male counterparts miss by being unable to watch and participate in the growth and development of their children. Fathers may not have to face a break in their career growth, but they do give up the wonder and challenge of being a part of a child's early years. Their absence from their children's development is a real loss to them and to the children. It's important to evaluate and accept the trade-off. We must realize that it is possible for us to have it all — a family and a career — but probably not at the same time. These are difficult choices. Our society has not yet faced the problem squarely, and has not begun to offer acceptable solutions for either sex.

Burnout: a risk for the unwary

For any woman seeking a leadership role, planning and conscious discipline are required to maintain a modicum of balance among family, friends, and a demanding career. The women who do it best exercise both discipline and a certain degree of self-indulgence. "Lunches are for friends, not business. I go to work early, I often work late, but for one or two hours in the middle of the day, I devote myself to friends and the interests we share." "Tuesday nights are for family, and Friday nights are just for my husband and me. No matter what." "When I feel myself getting crazy, I just leave the office and go work out. I'm so much better mentally when I've had some hard physical exercise." "I make myself take vacations. It sometimes seems impossible, but I take the time anyway. I've learned I'm much more effective if I take just a week or two completely away from business."

For women who don't achieve a balance, who let career become the number one priority to the exclusion of all other interests, the results can be disastrous. We've read about teacher burnout and burnout among health care providers. Now the problem is coming home to roost among the superachievers and workaholics who have given themselves wholeheartedly to advancing in their careers.

One woman in our group recently talked to us about her own experiences with burnout, a phenomenon that is just beginning to attract the attention it deserves in the business world. She told us how much she loved her job, and that if anyone had suggested to her that she might ever lose interest, she'd have laughed. Her greatest pleasure was work, and her constant obsession was meeting new challenges and achieving new levels of success. Yet she suddenly found herself unable to concentrate, disinterested, working only by rote. Because she had been financially successful, she was able to consider leaving her position when the opportunity presented itself. She traveled for a while, but felt aimless, bored, and exhausted. She was totally unable to focus on a new career, or to decide what she wanted to do with the rest of her life. Finally, out of financial necessity, she pulled herself together and began to consider options. She decided on an entrepeneurial career, because there would be lots of variety and she felt she could control her direction and the level of commitment to her work.

This woman defines burnout as "the loss of enthusiasm in one's job or career due to overload, either the company overloading you or you overloading yourself." She identifies the causes as "a big emphasis on 'making it' or proving something, a compulsive desire to succeed, a genuine love of work to the point of obsession, and lack of other interests." Symptoms of impending burnout are "*always* working late and on holidays, letting work become the main event of your life, having trouble unwinding so that you're always thinking about work, finding activities that used to be pleasurable (theater, family visits) becoming a chore, canceling social engagements or arriving late, losing touch with old friends, being relieved when your mate works late so that you won't be criticized for doing the same thing, and being almost addicted to stress so that on a 'normal' day you feel let down." In her case, when burnout finally occurred, our friend says she found herself "being dissatisfied with rewards, with no enthusiasm for anything, disillusioned with management, bored with everything, taking longer lunches, being late to work, feeling a vacuum in my life and having no idea what could fill it."

Our friend suggests that people who are "obsessive and tense about things," as she is, are more susceptible to burnout than are others who are less driven. She proposes as precautions against burnout, "better time management, learning to delegate, pacing yourself, pursuing new social interests and becoming involved in them, renewing old friendships, regaining your perspective, and reassessing your goals."

We discussed the differences between burnout and career transition. In one case a person may become bored with a particular career or profession and totally lose interest in it, or perhaps her area of specialization will prove to be a dead end, or her potential for future progress in her career will be severely constrained. Obviously this is a time of great frustration and worry, especially if the career is one for which the woman has spent years in schooling or special training. Yet the possibility exists to move on from the career that has proven stultifying, and to choose another, more rewarding path. In our fast-changing, technologically-oriented society this may happen several times, so that a person has three or four separate careers in a working lifetime. This situation is quite different from true burnout, where the individual loses interest not only in a particular career, but in any kind of work, and even in life itself. Burnout might even be considered a form of stress-related illness, in this case manifesting itself in mental exhaustion and boredom instead of in physical symptoms.

SUPPORT FROM OTHER WOMEN

Even when we take care to avoid burnout, the time constraints imposed on most working women expose us to alienation and loneliness that can become severe. We work through lunch, or we do our shopping, or we rush the cat to the vet. After work, if we leave on time, we may have a parent-teacher conference, or a child's dental appointment, or dinner to prepare. Weekends are spent cooking and shopping for the following week or — even more exciting — doing the laundry. Once family obligations are met and crises resolved, there is very little time to develop personal relationships or to pursue a social life. This is especially true in single-parent households. Many upwardly mobile women admit that the first sacrifice to their careers is an active social life and the reinforcement of friends. Some women pay for an hour with a psychiatrist simply as a substitute for the more time-consuming luxury of unloading on a friend.

We hope that groups such as Women in Management will provide increasing support for other women striving for leadership positions. They certainly offer a constructive, focused (and cheaper!) alternative to traditional group psychotherapy. Women's networks, both formal groups and informal "old girls' networks," can provide enormous reinforcement. This is an age-old habit with men, but a relatively new concept for most women. Networks give us an opportunity to sort out our ideas and to talk with people who share our interests. They provide not only reinforcement but also, in a sense, verification of our own worth. Many of us spend so much time working to achieve success that we become virtually isolated in terms of comparing ideas, considering cultural mores, and developing social attitudes. The intensity of our jobs precludes the outside stimulation that would come from ordinary social contact. A networking group, whose members experience the same career pressures, challenges, and frustrations, can both stimulate new ideas and help us evaluate existing situations. The exchange among women can help us get a clearer picture of our own developing thoughts. It can provide a shortcut to the maturing of ideas through trial and error by substituting the experience and insights of others.

Women who have already achieved success have an opportunity to provide support by acting as mentors for those who follow. And those of us acting as mentors can have not only the satisfaction of helping younger women move ahead, but also the gratification of learning from them and broadening our own horizons. In pushing those we help, we also stretch ourselves. "I never leave one of these sessions without an intellectual 'doggy bag.' I always take home something to chew on."

One reason that our Women in Management group has been so successful is our insistence on the informal structure, with no leader and no guest lecturers. Women have a tendency to be intimidated in those situations and to defer to the authority of "the expert." They won't ask questions or assert opinions, but will let themselves be talked at, ascribing expertise to the lecturer who often knows less from real-life experience than the women in the audience. We find that the pragmatic knowledge of our women is our greatest resource. Each of us knows something well enough to share it and thereby help the others. We wouldn't feel this privilege of sharing in a formal lecture situation.

We have talked in our group about men having more experience than we do at being "team players." It's a skill we certainly can and should learn, focusing on the good of the group and of other individuals within the group, rather than on what's best for us in particular. Men are also more accustomed than we are to supporting one another in their aspirations. On the whole, women's financial institutions (for example, women's banks that are established and run by women to encourage women in general to become independent borrowers and to provide other financial services) have failed to muster support from the constituents for whom they were developed. Supporting other women, rather than viewing them as competition or fearing their inexperience in a new role, can strengthen our organizations and ourselves. Opening avenues of communication and trust through women's networks is an excellent way to start supporting other women — and to encourage them to support us.

One of the most gratifying results of our WIM group's interaction is the way our women have started to use each other's professional expertise. Our entrepreneurs utilize the professional services of our lawyers, public relations consultants, accountants, bankers, etc., while some of the professional women have been inspired by the entrepreneurs to consider setting up their own professional practices. Many of us are thus in the position of admiring, encouraging, and actually *using* the skills other women in the group have to offer.

We decided that, as a group, WIM members should work very hard to change the attitude of women toward each other. We are convinced that it is imperative for women to see that supporting others of their own sex, instead of fearing their competition or their lack of experience as they move into new areas of responsibility, can actually strengthen our organizations and ourselves. Opening avenues of communication and trust through women's networks is an excellent way to begin supporting other women and to encourage them to support one another.

SEVEN

Mixing Business with Family

How Do I Relate?

CAN I WORK WITH MEMBERS OF MY FAMILY?

Several of the women in our group work with family members: husbands, sisters and brothers, children, parents. On the one hand, it seems natural, desirable, and economically advantageous to start a business with family members as partners or subordinates, or to break into the business world through an existing family business. On the other hand, working with family has many perils that don't exist in other business relationships. For example, problems at work can spill over into problems at home, and vice versa; close family ties can work strange magic on business communication and lines of authority; and conflicting styles and sensitive egos can totally disrupt efficient operations.

In our group discussions we have shared our own approaches and techniques for coping with the problems of extending close family ties into the work environment. We have been interested in learning more about how other "family companies" work. Two of our members took on the assignment of researching the topic and leading a discussion group about their findings — and about their personal experiences in working in a family business.

Do family businesses work?

Since we'd heard the old maxims about separating personal life

from business, and the warnings about nepotism being an ex-
cuse for incompetence, it seemed likely that family businesses
would be in the minority. Our research turned up a couple of
real surprises. First, the psychology journals weren't filled with
studies of the problems of family members who work together.
But business publications had a lot to offer on the successes of
family businesses. The statistics were astonishing: 980,000 out
of 1,000,000 corporations in the United States are family
dominated; 95 percent of all business units, 99 percent of construction firms, 88 percent of construction sales firms, 96 percent of retail distribution firms, 94 percent of wholesale firms,
70 percent of wholesale sales firms, 94 percent of manufacturing firms, and 30 percent of manufacturing sales firms are pri-
vately held family-owned businesses. The 50 *largest* industrial
firms are family owned![6] Clearly, whatever the problems of
working with family, there must be ways to solve them successfully.

Why it's tough to work with family
Problems in our own experience are probably typical. Some
are generated within the family relationship itself. "You have
one role, one set of expectations, at home and another role,
another set of expectations, at work. Your expectation that
Mama will take care of you and make everything wonderful
just doesn't apply when you're in business together." "I had always thought we could put our heads together and come up
with a solution, but when it came to our business, we couldn't
agree. For me, his agreeing was all tied up with approval and
support, and suddenly I realized I had to stand on my own and
not back away from what I thought was right, even when he
disapproved of it." "When my son came into the business, I
thought 'at last, someone to support my ideas.' Of course I'm
finding out that isn't true." "I can't let myself hurry him. I'm
the older sister, and I still feel in a position of authority toward
him. But now I have to wait and let him finish thinking it
through, and allow him to express his opinion." "Sometimes
you just have to learn to ignore the automatic assumptions of
authority associated with family roles. In business you can't
say, 'I'm the mother and you're the child.' "

Not all problems arise from internal stresses. Some are imposed from the outside. One of our members experienced directly the pressures placed on a child entering a family business with a successful parent. "There was a certain set of expectations imposed on her by people outside the business. She just didn't have the same freedom to make mistakes and learn from them that a stranger would have had. Carrying our name was a double whammy: she not only had to learn the business, but she also had to live up to what other people expected of her just because she belonged to our family."

Some problems in working with family members arise from our traditional roles as women. "I'm very involved with my family financially, but I don't work with them. My father and brother work together, but they won't work with me because they don't respect me. It has a lot to do with my being the only girl in the family, and it's very difficult for me."

Still other problems are peculiar to married couples. "I found that when my husband and I worked together, spent all day together at the office, we came home at night and had nothing to talk about. I had to move out of the office, move out of the building; we now see one another only at home in the evenings, and that's much better for us." "There are turf problems, and ego problems, but we've learned not to fall apart. We each have different strengths, and they complement one another. We've separated our responsibilities to take advantage of what each of us does best. When he infringes on my turf, I growl, and he does the same to me." Not all marriages withstand the strains. One of our women, in business with her husband, saw their marriage end in divorce. Yet she and her former husband are still in a successful real estate development partnership. "We couldn't do it and live together," she says. Still, both were totally committed to the business. Without the strains of the marriage, they've been able to enjoy a profitable business relationship.

What seems universal in family businesses is that because the ties are deeper than in ordinary working relationships, the problems are more acute. "In a family business, the cuts are always deeper and the blood redder." "Sometimes the family relationship is used in business to make people do things they don't want to do. 'We're a family, we have to stick together' sometimes means 'It's my idea. You all follow me off the cliff, because I don't think *your* idea is any good!' "

Grievances are common in all employee/employer relationships, but when they occur in a family business they can inflict special pain. "Many conflicts in family businesses are caused by lack of communication. There is a surplus of thoughtless, vain, overbearing, misleading, dishonest talk, and never enough earnestness and honesty," one of our women says. Another recognizes, "I'm a lot more blunt with my sister than I am with any other employee. I don't use tact with her, and I'll have to learn to do that if we're going to stay together. I can't be the big sister telling her what to do. She just ignores me when I take that tone, something she'd never do with an employer. She gets defensive and I get mad."

Making a go of a family business

While we have a pretty representative sampling in our group of the problems of working with family members, we also have a handle on some solutions: approaches that have been successful in keeping members of our group working effectively and happily with parents, siblings, children, or spouses. We've learned that it *can* work wonderfully well, but that it's never easy and it takes continual conscious effort. In fact, keeping a family business running smoothly is just as hard as keeping a marriage and family on the right track. The same kinds of trade-offs are required, and each family member must consciously give to the relationship. Everyone in the family business must be committed to making it work. A high degree of tolerance is essential, along with deep respect for one another.

What makes family business particularly difficult is the tendency we all have to take our workday problems home. When parents and married children are in business together, this natural reaction can cause problems that never come up when the family and business relationships are separate. One example from our group was related by a member whose husband and son work together in a very successful enterprise. Both contribute to the success of the business, and their disparate talents complement one another. Each recognizes and respects the other's contributions. But when they occasionally disagree on some issue regarding the company's direction, their arguments can become heated. The son tends to take his anger home, and to vent his resentments to his wife, painting a terrible picture of his father's unfairness and his stubborn insistence on the "wrong" decision for their company. Naturally, his wife supports his position and resents the unjust treatment her husband is receiving from her father-in-law. Within a day or two the father and son have worked out their differences satisfactorily, but the wife is still seething at her in-laws. Naturally her husband has forgotten to tell her that all is well, and she is still feeling protective of him when next the family gets together. Her anger and resentment, which have been growing, are apparent in her cool demeanor, and the entire family feels the strain.

This transfer of emotion from business to family, and the imperfect communication it represents, is a typical problem in family-owned businesses. It's particularly common where a younger member of the family, still feeling a little insecure in his or her own abilities, needs strokes and reinforcement from a spouse and uses the tactic of blaming insensitive parents as a means to gain emotional support. It's not just the younger member who can create problems in a parent/child business venture. Parents can sometimes be so eager for a child to succeed in the family business that they protect him or her from the consequences of errors that are part of the normal learning experience. It takes the child longer to learn and to feel self-confident than it would in the normal course of trial and error.

In any family business, open communication and trust among *all* the family members, not just those actually involved in the business, can help to strengthen the relationship and to avoid dangerous pitfalls in both the business and the family. One example of how this can work comes from a woman in our group who is in a very successful venture capital business with her son. She started the business and invited him to join her when he turned 30. They agreed to a three-year trial: if it didn't work out during that time, she would continue the business and he'd still be young enough to try something new. Her one condition was that both her son and his wife must be in total accord about launching the business. She recognized that her daughter-in-law was a key to their survival; without her support, the business couldn't make it. The daughter-in-law bought in totally. The painful surprise was the lack of enthusiasm and support from friends and other family members who predicted failure, terrible family strains, and the probable alienation of mother and son.

The business has just celebrated its tenth anniversary, and continues to grow and prosper, as does the son's marriage. The partners are still good friends. And so are the mother and daughter-in-law. The mother speculates that the most important ingredient in their success was probably the strong desire of both partners for the business to make it, if only to show their detractors how wrong they were. They also had healthy respect for each other, plus appreciation for the expertise and professionalism that each brought to the business. Outside the office they were mother and son; inside they were professional equals. No matter how much they argued and disagreed in the process of reaching any business decision, each supported it 100 percent once the commitment was made. If the decision proved wrong, they didn't waste time in recriminations, but set about using their combined energies to "fix it," and to prevent damage to the business. At times there were tremendous strains on both the business and the personal relationships, but after 10 years the mother is willing to bet they'll make it.

Another of our women points out the different stages in the life of a family business. "In the early days, when it's a struggle to make ends meet and just making the business go takes every bit of energy you have, you don't really have time for ego problems. It's later, when you begin staking out specific territories, that you start to infringe on one another. Then you have to find a way to define and accept those boundary lines, or you can't keep working together." It helps to bring different expertise to the business. "We have cut out the area where we think he is strong, and the area where I'm the stronger, and that's how we divide our responsibilities. After all the years we've been married, I'm astonished that working together like this has been an enriching experience. I find I'm discovering him as a person, learning totally unexpected things about him." Intimate knowledge of a family member's strengths and weaknesses can be a benefit. "You can get more out of a family member because you know what he wants to do. You can give him a position doing what he does best, then let him grow with it." Accepting the assigned roles is also of critical importance. "We have made our line of demarcation. He makes the decisions and I implement them. He creates it, I run it." "We have true peer equality, so we've just parceled out the work according to which of us is better at each part of it. It isn't a status thing, it's just efficient."

Our women who work with family all urge one thing: differentiate what is business and what is family. Don't assume that one role carries over into the other. Enjoy encouraging growth and self-confidence in children, siblings, or spouse. Appreciate the ability to trust completely in the honesty of a business associate with whom you have a special family relationship. It's also a special opportunity for you to flourish, knowing that he or she is eager for you to succeed and do your best.

Establishing ground rules at the beginning can save a lot of grief later on. One member of our group says "We've applied the advice we got from a lawyer about working with friends. He said, 'Put everything on paper first; that way you can keep your friendship.' First you spell out what the working arrangement will be so that everyone understands. Then you can stay close as a family. When the business details are taken care of first, you protect your personal relationship." Another agrees. "I'm the one who always insists on legal details. When we haven't bothered, but have gotten by on the basis of a spoken agreement, we always wind up with an emotional conflict. It's probably more important to put it in writing when family is involved than when you're dealing with a stranger." One of our women entrepreneurs ignored this rule when her brother-in-law "generously" stepped in and offered financial backing for her new venture. Two years and a nasty lawsuit later, she is starting another new business—because her brother-in-law wound up with the last one. "I'll never again shake hands on a deal because 'it's all in the family'!"

Even when the agreement isn't legal, our members believe

it is important to set guidelines. It's especially important to expose children to the ins and outs of the work world so that one
day they may enter it as equals. "We started making clear rules
about appropriate business conduct when the children were
very young. After we gave them our rules, we had them write
some of their own. These included some things they would
never do at the office, such as 'no pinching, biting, or scratch-
ing.' " "Many of the people who work for me have toddlers or
infants. They are with us at work most of the time, and they
participate in some of the simple things that need to be done.
It's extremely valuable for the kids to be exposed to work."
"I've hired my 15-year-old to help me with the income tax. He
does certain specific tasks, and he's been very receptive and
very professional. If something isn't done just right, I give it
back to him. I haven't heard a word of complaint; he just goes
and does it the right way. When I compare this with trying to
get him to do something in the yard or around the house, it's
a totally different attitude."

Finally, our women warn that no one entering a family business relationship should have false expectations that it's going
to be easy. "To expect it to be comfortable and pleasant all the
time is unrealistic. Sometimes relationships are stressful and
abrasive, and occasionally that's very constructive. If you have
the basic sense of loving one another despite the business
conflicts, you can grow stronger as a result of the clashes."
"There's something in the fact that our relationship is secure;
no matter how much we disagree, there will never be a time
when he is not my brother, or I am not his sister. We can disagree, but our disagreement won't end the relationship."
"Communication is the key to any working relationship."

Words of wisdom for family businesses

The women who studied family businesses as a research
project for the group found two important rules reflected in the
literature. First, get outside experience before joining a family
firm. (Some businesses approach this formally. The Associated
General Contractors of America has a project of swapping
sons and daughters among noncompetitive construction firms
for periods up to five years.) Second, be aware of the personal

relationships involved in your family business and don't allow them to override good business practices; set up programs to protect against this. (Some of the specific programs outlined by the contractors' association include having outsiders on your board, setting up good audit and review procedures, and bringing in outside consultants to evaluate management and to set goals.)

[6]Statistics courtesy of The Center for Family Business, Cleveland, Ohio, 1983.

PART THREE

WOMEN IN ENTREPRENEURSHIP

Let's start by defining entrepreneurship, or rather by selecting the definition that seems most appropriate to the women about whom we're writing. First of all, we know that entrepreneurship means more than just starting a business.

Joseph Schumpeter saw entrepreneurs as "reform[ing] or revolutioniz[ing] the pattern of production by exploiting an invention or, more generally, an untried technological possibility."[7] Robert Hisrich defines it as "the process of creating something different with value by devoting the necessary time and effort, assuming the accompanying financial, psychological, and social risks, and receiving the resulting rewards of monetary and personal satisfaction."[8]

In his definition, George Kozmetsky urges consideration of the fact that the modern entrepreneur doesn't exist in a vacuum. Contemporary entrepreneurship, he says, is a linking together of "1. talent (people); 2. technology (ideas); 3. capital (resources); and 4. know-how (knowledge). Entrepreneurial talent consists of special types of individuals—people who make things happen. Entrepreneurs are individuals who recognize opportunities and are willing to take individual risks."[9]

Entrepreneurship has also been called America's secret

weapon for individual economic success, and for many of the women in our group that has certainly been the case. In examining the challenges and opportunities for women who strive for top leadership positions, our group has focused heavily on entrepreneurship as presenting a unique opportunity for women to escape some of the factors limiting their advance to the very top ranks in the corporate world.

We know that entrepreneurial women are an increasingly significant phenomenon in our society. We want to know more: who *are* these daring women, and what motivates them to break away from the herd?

Being possessed of that strong female characteristic, practicality, we also want to take a look at the nuts and bolts of entrepreneurship. Assuming that the creativity and drive exist, where does a woman get the money to start her own business? What can she do to protect herself financially early in the life of her business? What happens if the business fails? What are the actual steps in getting the business started? Once it's launched, how does she get it moving toward survival and, eventually, success?

We aren't content with definitions or with philosophical possibilities for women in entrepreneurship. We want details!

---

[7]Joseph Schumpeter, *Can Capitalism Survive?* (New York: Harper and Row, 1952),

[8]Robert D. Hisrich, *Entrepreneurship, Intrapreneurship, and Venture Capital: The Foundation of Economic Renaissance* (Lexington, Mass., and Toronot, Canada: D.C. Heath & Co., 1986),

[9]George Kozmetsky, "Entrepreneurial Growth and Austin's Future" (speech presented at Chamber of Commerce meeting, Austin, Texas, January 1988).

EIGHT

The Entrepreneur

Should I Be on My Own?

DO I HAVE THE MAKINGS OF AN ENTREPRENEUR?

In our group we talk a lot about entrepreneurs: people who go out and start their own businesses, then build and manage them; or, perhaps, people who get them going, sell out, and move on to some other new enterprise. What distinguishes such people from those who build their careers in a corporate setting and continue to grow into senior management positions? Or from those who come up through the ranks of government or academic institutions to become top political leaders or university presidents? Are entrepreneurs in fact different — or do they just find themselves in different situations? Some of us who are attracted to "doing our own thing" have turned to more experienced members of the group for advice, and maybe a little encouragement.

The special new phenomenon of women in entrepreneurial roles is of growing importance in our society. One of our women attended a White House conference to which 70 or 80 top women entrepreneurs had been invited. President Ronald Reagan informed the elite group that there are currently three million women entrepreneurs in the United States; one in four businesses is owned by a woman. And in the areas of finance and high technology, there has been a 97 percent growth rate in the number of businesses owned by women. Clearly, women entrepreneurs are a force to be reckoned with.

We started examining entrepreneurs by looking at a few basic reasons why either men or women would choose an entrepreneurial role: they become dissatisfied with their current employment; they recognize an opportunity; they feel an urge to try a new venture; a change in public policy opens up a new possibility; they can't resist trying out an innovative idea; they have no alternative if they want to maintain a desired standard of living.[10] Which of these reasons applied to *our* women entrepreneurs? Or did all of them?

For a few women in our group there was really no question about being on their own. "I had finally reached the point where I couldn't stand the thought of working another day for anyone else. I just couldn't take it. I had to start my own business." "With that kind of drive you don't even consider the demands that will be made on you. You just can't wait to get started." "I didn't have the option of staying at home and I knew I couldn't work for anyone else, so I had to start my own business. At first I didn't know what the business would be, but six weeks later I opened the doors of my first duplicating shop. Now, after 11 years, I have nine shops, I'm chairman of the board, I'm going to retire this year and take two years off to travel. Then I'm going to start my own consulting practice." "I didn't know a thing about running a business, but I knew I wanted to run one."

Not all of us who wind up starting or managing our own businesses are quite so driven or so successful, but as a group we felt we could identify the traits that our entrepreneurial members shared with other entrepreneurs that we knew.

Most entrepreneurs, especially entrepreneurial women, demonstrate particularly well-developed characteristics that we've described earlier as typical of successful women: they have strong survival aptitudes, and they have high energy levels. Low-energy women can't make it as entrepreneurs; they won't have enough time to do everything that has to be done. As we've already noted, there is a close correlation between energy level and time management. Women who have low energy usually also have low survival efficiency. They manage their time poorly; each task takes so much time that they run out of time and energy before the tasks are finished. High-energy women are highly efficient and often highly successful.

Entrepreneurs are risk takers

We see entrepreneurs as people who commit themselves fully to achieving their goals where others might take a slower, and apparently more secure, route to career advancement. "These are hard-driving people who are not afraid to take risks." "They are active, not passive, types, and prefer to participate." "They will take risks nobody else would take. A true entrepreneur takes chances almost automatically." "People who are truly entrepreneurs don't theorize for a long time — they do it!" "There are going to be times when you have an opportunity and you have less than half an hour to make up your mind. If you wait until you have all the information, your chance will be gone. You have to be ready to act with almost no information." "True entrepreneurs are blissful in their sense of being able to accomplish their goals. They don't hear the world around them saying 'No you can't.' " "It's either easy for you to take chances or you just can't do it." "You can't divorce goals from risk taking." "They just never think about 'job security.' " "Their whole attitude is 'go for broke.' " "An entrepreneur will risk going bankrupt to be his or her own boss." "The entrepreneur says, 'I have a terrific idea. Let's do it!' and never looks back."

One feeling our group shares is that the whole question of risk taking is different for women than for men. It's also different for married women than for single women; different for single parents than for childless single women; and different for women who have financial backing from some source — parents, a spouse, a generous divorce settlement — than for those who are strictly on their own. It's far easier to take risks when you have someone or something to fall back on. And it seems to be easier for men, in general, to take risks than for women in similar situations. For example, a married man who risks an established career to start his own business usually has his wife as a support person. If his great idea fizzles, he can pick himself up, look on his experience as something valuable, and move on with his career. A woman who tries and fails, even with the financial and moral support of a spouse, is usually not so resilient as her male counterpart, and her career is seldom unaffected. The experience of failure shakes her self-confidence. If she does resume her former career path, she may find herself returning to corporate life in a diminished capacity. Even if she doesn't suffer the humiliation of a reduction in earnings and status, she has greatly damaged her own feelings of self-worth — an attitude far less common among men.

Because of these real cultural and emotional differences, women have been poorly represented among the ranks of entrepreneurs in this country until very recently. The new woman entrepreneur is, indeed, one of a special breed. The reluctance women have felt to start their own businesses has in part reflected lack of start-up capital available to women. It has also reflected an intense fear of failure. It is encouraging to see that women today are beginning to recognize that failure is *not* a fatal condition. As a group, women are increasingly taking on business challenges and risking the pitfalls of business ownership rather than settling for security.

An entrepreneur's business is the most important thing in the world

Are you willing to work 60 or 80 hours a week without wages for long periods of time with no assurance of success? If you're an entrepreneur, you don't even have to think about it. Your business is "almost an obsession," one of our women says; others would seriously question the "almost"! This is how some of our entrepreneurs see themselves and their situations. "It's not so much that you think putting in your 80 hours a week is a neat part of it. It's your commitment." "You can work 70 hours a week for somebody else and not get a single thrill out of that. Working 70 hours a week for yourself seems like 12." One woman summed the matter up neatly: "You've got to have the stamina."

For entrepreneurs, it isn't just long hours and hard work that take a toll. The business is always foremost in their minds. "Entrepreneurs generally don't sleep worth a darn. We lie awake and worry a whole lot." "My sleep is so interrupted. I wake up worrying all the time. I call old friends in the middle of the night." "My business is on my mind a lot more than my husband or my child. I think about my partner more than I think about my husband." "You end up having less freedom to come and go, but you don't mind it because it's such a thrill to be doing it." "The highlight of my month is getting the statement back from my accountant. It's due Wednesday, and if I don't have it by Thursday, I'm on the phone, saying, 'Just tell me the numbers.' I want to know so badly. Did I make money this month? If I'm in trouble, I want to know it fast so I can turn it around next month."

Financial awareness is essential

While women entrepreneurs, no less than men, must be risk takers, they are usually more sensitive to the downside of financial risks in what they do. Most women in our culture learn early in their adult lives to live within constrained financial limits. Early on they must manage their households to conform to their financial situations. They learn to budget to survive. (One of our women describes going to a lecture on linear programming some years ago, and making a rather deflating remark. When the lecture was over, she said, "Big deal; linear programming is just household budgeting. I've had to do that ever since I got married.") This built-in sense of making do on a shoestring gives women a perspective on business finance different from that of most men.

Cost effectiveness and cash flow are keenly watched by women entrepreneurs. Two of our women who launched a service business watched it get off to a slow start, mostly because of a sluggish economy in their community. They watched their cash flow like a pair of hawks and at one point, when the situation became critical, they canceled their paid janitorial service and took on the work themselves to cut costs. As their situation has improved, they've been able to contract again for a cleaning service, but their willingness to go the extra mile and take on that additional (and very nonexecutive) task is typical of the way women entrepreneurs approach their businesses. In part this stems from the budgeting habit, deeply ingrained in most women who have had to manage a household. It often reflects, as well, the fact that women entrepreneurs almost always have less financial support than men in similar circumstances. Bankers and other investors still find it difficult to make loans to women whose businesses get into a "cash crunch." Women are acutely aware of this disparity and live in fear of getting caught short. Also women, by training and acculturation, absolutely abhor debt. As our owner-janitors demonstrated, they will go to extremes to avoid excessive debt in business dealings. This comes naturally to those of us who grew up in the days when two-income families were the exception rather than the rule, and may well hang on in the daughters of women who grew up in that era. At that time, the male head-of-household was the sole provider, and the wife typically managed the household on a fixed amount doled out weekly or monthly. She learned to manipulate those dollars amazingly well to be sure they'd stretch to cover all the family's needs, including unanticipated emergencies. "Cash flow" was a daily reality for most women, and making available dollars fit real needs was a truly creative endeavor.

One of our women, assessing qualities necessary to a successful entrepreneur, stressed the need for financial savvy. "As an entrepreneur it is essential that you have reasonably good ability to deal with finances. If you try to delegate that to somebody else, it's not going to work. I think that's one of the very critical areas in which you must have some competence." Another member says, feelingly, "Nobody cares about your money as much as you do!"

Entrepreneurs want full credit — and blame

Entrepreneurs by nature want to be in charge of the whole show. They want to make the decisions, and face the consequences. "I enjoy doing it my way. When everybody else is making right turns, I always say, 'What if I turn left? What if I go straight instead?' It is just this curiosity, what if I do this, what will happen? When I make a turn, it could be successful." "I wanted to do something that is strictly mine; to have full and total control." "When entrepreneurs make their choices they know they can't blame someone else. They have full responsibility." "My business is very service oriented. What can make or break you is your interface with the client.

If you have a hired employee who works 8:00 to 5:00, and when that clock hits 5:00 you have a client waiting out there, the employee is not going to put in a minute of extra time. It has to be you out there, you being obsessed with the clients and being sure they're getting the quality of service you have promised." "Part of the thrill is producing something that is on the market, and having total control over the design and how it is done." If you're an entrepreneurial type, this focus on your business doesn't seem excessive. It's the way things are, and were always meant to be!

Message to entrepreneurs: Know thyself!

Starting a business is a learning experience, no matter what you take into it. One of our successful entrepreneurs said, "You have to recognize your own strengths and weaknesses. You have to be ready to seek advice to fill in all your own gaps. You've got to have the ability to fly by the seat of your pants, but you've also got to know when and where to get help. Your education going into it doesn't make a lot of difference, but if your education doesn't continue and escalate dramatically when you get into your own business, you're going to be in a whole lot of trouble."

One of our women entrepreneurs had struggled for years to build a very successful business. Recently, when things finally seemed secure and the business was at a new peak, she decided to sell the majority share in her company to her employees, and to let the new employee-owners take over management. Naturally, this surprised many of us. She explained that she had come to realize over the years that her real talent (and enthusiasm) lay in conceiving and developing a business. When it came to running an established business, she had neither the motivation, nor the specific skills, to nurture and refine it. Why not turn it over to the employees who had helped build it and now owned a large part of it? After all, they had new incentive to make it grow and continue to prosper. The woman who assumed the managerial role had been a key employee for many years, yet she could never have launched the business as our entrepreneurial member did. Her skills are totally different. We've watched with interest and have seen that our member's expectations have been realized. Under the leadership of the new manager, the business is expanding steadily. While there haven't been many innovations introduced, the business has opened several subsidiary operations and its shareholders, our member *and* the employee-owners, are beneficiaries of this growth. The different, but equally significant, creative talents of the entrepreneur and of the manager have brought the business to its full potential.

Our friend made another very significant point about leaving her business. "The energy and drive necessary to build a new business and propel it to success have to come from a desperate need. I think one reason that a huge percentage of all new businesses fail is that the entrepreneurs who start them haven't reached the point of desperation before they launch their businesses. When I recognized, after many years, that the needs that had driven me to start my business had been met, I realized that I no longer needed the business, and it didn't need me. Then it was time to get out, before the business or I suffered the consequences. You and the business have to be satisfying a real need in each other if the chemistry is going to work."

Interestingly, this woman has recently launched a new and totally different entrepreneurial venture. From a service-oriented business, she has moved into the area of retail sales. It will be fun to see how the new business grows and develops. We look forward to seeing how she'll meet the very different, but equally demanding, challenges of her new environment. "All I can say for certain," she says at this point, "is that I know my real interest and talent lies in developing new businesses. I look forward to applying what I've learned from my first entrepreneurial career, and to learning the ins and outs of this new world."

Knowing, as our friend did, when to leave a company she has started can be one of the toughest decisions an entrepreneur can make. In our Women in Management meetings, we've talked about the possibility that this "sacrifice" may be easier for a woman than for a man, culturally accustomed as we have been to setting our own desires aside in favor of those of our husbands and children. Does our history of making unselfish choices give us an edge? Is this a secret advantage women entrepreneurs can exploit, making the right kind of tough choices, out of habit, that will in the long run benefit our companies? Letting go of a company is not unlike raising a child to be independent and self-sustaining, and watching that child leave the nest. If parents have done a good job, they will let go, the child will grow away from them naturally, and will begin to make a life of her or his own. Extending the analogy, we might say the most successful companies are those that remain whole and productive while they generate many successful spin-off operations.

---

[10] George Kozmetsky, "Entrepreneurial Growth and Austin's Future" (speech presented at Chamber of Commerce meeting, Austin, Texas, January 1988).

NINE

Financing My Own Business

Where Do I Turn?

WHERE DO I GO FOR FINANCING?
Having a pretty good handle on the characteristics of entrepreneurs and how we match up, we can begin to concentrate on where a woman entrepreneur might turn for funding to get a new business off the ground. Assuming one of us has the drive to start her own business, is eager to take the risk, willing to put the business first without question, and happy to take full responsibility for the results, she still has the problem of capital: gathering enough money to get the business off the ground without dooming it to automatic failure because of insufficient early funding. Some lucky entrepreneurs have personal funds or family financing that enables them to start their businesses without having to seek outside money. Most of us, though, have to figure out what we'll need to launch our new ventures and then persuade someone to back us. As we have seen within our group, this is a new experience for most women, and, at least at first, a particularly difficult one.

How much is enough?
The first question we have to face is how much capital do we really need to get a business off the ground and then to see it through the initial stages? For some businesses we must plan

ahead to accommodate expansion, or to get through a heavy seasonal inventory investment, or to allow for adding personnel. For others, particularly those that are oriented toward a service rather than a product, it may be possible to start with a very modest investment in facilities and equipment and then expand only when the business generates sufficient income to support growth.

Our discussions suggested that the question of how much is enough, like so many others, has a different answer for a man starting a new business than for a woman in the same situation. Men seem to be less concerned with month-to-month earnings than are women. If there is a slow month, a man's first thought is to borrow enough to tide the business over until next month; a woman, whose whole orientation is toward budgeting, is inclined to look on borrowing as a last resort. (As one of our group said, "Housewives have *learned* to make do.") Women tend to think of money in finite terms: what you've got is the limit of what you can spend. Men are less constrained by immediate realities. Almost all our entrepreneurs told a similar story about early financing. "If a man takes a $100,000 loan to get started, a woman will take $25,000, if that much. We're much tighter in running our businesses." "A friend and I both started new businesses at about the same time our husbands did. We made bookshelves out of concrete blocks and boards, just as we had in college. Our office space cost about $25 a month, and she had a door for a desk, and I had an old desk of my father's. And here were our husbands in lovely offices, with modern equipment, and they didn't have any money either. But they'd taken out these loans."

"We tend to undercapitalize, to try to get by on less by being superhuman." "At least in the past, women going into business didn't have a heck of a chance of landing a $100,000 loan on guts and glory. We have a better chance now with women getting into the banking business, and more women having started on a shoestring and making it — showing we *can* pay back loans." "A change of attitude is extremely important for us right now. As our attitudes change, we can move much more quickly."

One of the women in the group asked the two members who

had started their businesses with the "make do" offices how
their enterprises had progressed in relation to their husbands'
businesses, which were fortified by bank loans. As it turned
out, all the businesses survived the start-up phase and are successful today. With their borrowed start-up capital, the men
were able to get off to a faster pace. The women's businesses
had a modest growth cycle and took longer to become self-
sustaining. On the other hand, the women were free of their
outside financial obligations far earlier than were their husbands, and they never had the heavy monthly payments their
husbands had to face. This is a good example of a point mentioned earlier: not having heavy debt-service costs can mean
healthier and more predictable cash flow, and can allow for
carefully paced growth.

Still, however much we pride ourselves on our ability to "get
by," undercapitalization is a major stumbling block for many
new businesses. The business can go just so far on start-up
capital and "sweat equity," and then it stagnates because
there's no money for expansion. Alternatively, "with a lot of
new businesses, when they get into a terrific expansion period,
they hit a cash crunch. So many people run like mad and make
a wonderful success, and then go bankrupt because they've
grown too fast." One of our members thought that the growth-
to-bankruptcy syndrome "may not happen so much with a
woman's business as with a man's because we are so damned
chicken and so conservative! We stay on such a shoestring because we don't have the guts to take a gamble." "I read a
newspaper article quoting a woman who advises women going
into business. She said that women entrepreneurs have a lower
failure rate than men because they are willing to make an ex-
traordinary commitment."

A compromise must be reached between extravagance and
being "too damned chicken." "You have to reach a sensible
balance between starting with everything and starting with
nothing. Walk the middle ground." "Even if you wanted a
$100,000 loan, you'd probably be so nervous you couldn't get
it, or take it if you did get it. At some point you have to stick
to your own style until you develop self-confidence." We
agreed you must adjust your financial goals as your business

situation changes. "We're willing to work for a time without salaries and to pour money back into the business, but at a certain point the business has to make money or we go on to something else." "We have monetary goals that have to be met. If we meet our goals, we continue." "You have to know what your bottom line is, whether you made money last month or lost it. In any new business, you'd better know that pretty darned fast or you can go broke." "I sometimes get to the point where I say 'If we can't buy this piece of equipment, or expand into one more room, is it worth it? Should we continue?' "

In assessing how much you need to start your business, make necessary purchases of equipment and inventory, hire staff or consultants, pay for various services, and survive several months — allowing for seasonal fluctuations in your particular business — a detailed business plan is essential. A three- to five-year plan, with at least the first year broken down by quarters, can help you see what you'll need and when. The business plan should show that between the money you are investing or have already raised, and what you're asking the lender to supply, you have enough capital on hand to cover all your costs, including personal living expenses, for a minimum of six months. Some advisors recommend that you take this figure and *multiply it by three* to be safe. A good business plan is also a guide against which to measure your performance, and it forms a basis for your subsequent financial reporting to the lender. We'll talk about business plans in more detail later in this chapter.

The advice of an accountant, and perhaps a lawyer and a financial consultant, can be invaluable as you plan for your needs. A professional advisor can help you determine the immediate and longer-range needs for capital, the impact of various types of financing on the new business, and the capacity of the business to discharge debts. This information can help to shape your decision about the type of financing optimal for your new business. The all-important question of where to find such advisors will be addressed later (see Chapter 10).

EXPLORING THE RESOURCES

In talking about sources of financing, we recognized that many women feel awkward trying to borrow money or to attract investors. First, it is difficult for them to believe that bankers or investors will be interested in what they are proposing. Without a track record of borrowing and repaying loans, or of starting and managing businesses, it's often hard for them to sell themselves and their ideas. And then they tend to feel committed to the first person they approach, as if it's somehow impolite or illegitimate to shop for the best deal. We explored likely sources of funding for new business ventures, the trade-offs of each, and how to get the best deal for ourselves. We talked about the importance of finding the right banker or investor to suit our particular needs and personal styles. Since our group includes bankers and private investors, as well as entrepreneurs and managers, we had a variety of perspectives on this question.

One of our problems seems to be feeling apologetic at having to borrow. "I think I felt I should be able to pick myself up by my bootstraps, but finally I did get to the point where I realized I couldn't do the kind of expansion I was thinking about without a bank loan." "This year, we've finally stopped financing the operation ourselves. We're starting to go for more traditional financing. We've gotten one bank loan and paid it back. Now we don't have to save a certain amount to start off the Christmas season. We get it financed."

One helpful suggestion from a banker in our group was to "establish a relationship with your banker *before* you need money." Another was to "understand the industry. Then you'll begin to see what loan officers need from you and how you can help them assess your business."

Borrowing from banks

A hurdle we must get over is embarrassment at our inexperience. "Sometimes we are hesitant to go into the bank and say, 'I don't know anything about bank loans. Would you explain to me what this is?' " "I'm trying to put together a business plan, and I know nothing about it. I've made a commitment for about $50,000 worth of equipment. The banker went over my business plan. We spent a good two hours so that he would understand what I am doing. Then he prepared the

loan paper for me, and I said, 'Let me think about it over-
night.' All I had to do was say, 'Yes, that's the amount I want.'
I know it's up to me. Deep down I know I am going forward,
but it's like I am having to be dragged kicking and screaming
through this. I've never taken out a bank loan before. I don't
know why it intimidates me."

One of our women saw our feminine need to relate to individuals as a stumbling block to getting the best possible
financing for our businesses. "If we talk to one banker, and he
or she is honest and helpful, we feel committed to that person
because we have established a relationship. I think this sort of
thing may be one of the difficulties that we women have in
translating into new environments. We are used to dealing
with people and developing a relationship of trust. That's how
we operate. But there are different deals being made, and we
should shop around at several banks to learn more about the
situation." Those experienced in borrowing — and lending —
agreed with her. "Anytime you are making a commitment you
need to compare different offers and alternatives." "You've got
to think of protecting yourself. If you wind up paying an extra
10 percent in interest, you may not be able to make your payments." "When I had to get my first loan I didn't know enough
to shop at several banks. Out of stupidity it turned out well for
me. I had a trust at one bank and a company account at
another, so, for the heck of it, I called the one where I had the
trust and I found out I had a bargaining package. I went back
and forth between them and I ended up getting a very good
deal." "It helps if you go in to a particular banker and say 'So-
and-so suggested I come talk to you.' It helps to open those
doors a little bit and lets you feel less intimidated. We *shouldn't*
feel intimidated; they're there for us." "Get the old-girl network
working for you. We've got it; flaunt it!"

Members of our group suggested another reason to shop
around. Not all loan officers carry equal weight. "Can the loan
officer you're talking to make that loan decision or does it have
to go through a committee? Find out, because the loan committee often will take a week or more and if you're in a time
crunch you need to know that." "As a borrower I learned you
absolutely must match your level of business expertise with

your banker's level. I got hung up with a young, inexperienced loan officer and she was not willing to take my case before the loan committee to defend it. I wound up having to pull rank and go straight to the chairman of the board and the chairman of the loan committee to talk about my situation. Then everything was fine, because they understood what I was doing. Make sure the banker you are dealing with has the business acumen to understand the types of projects you are working on." "Don't hesitate to change bankers, even in the same organization. Be sure you are on the same wavelength. It's like a doctor, attorney, or anything else. If you don't get along, or if they don't understand your business, then you have the wrong person." "Talk to several at once. Play one against the other. Why be ashamed? That's business."

A compelling reason to shop was offered by a banker in the group. She said, "Don't trade flexibility for pricing. Don't try to get the cheapest deal. Try to get the deal that lets *you* — not the banker — run your business."

Those who have been through it before can be very encouraging. "Until my husband died, and I inherited the software business, I had always been a housewife at home raising my children. I'd never run a business, and I'd certainly never applied for a loan. I'm finding a change in me. Where I was afraid, I am not afraid anymore. About three years to the day after his death, I went down to the bank to borrow $150,000. These things don't bother me now. I don't have time."

Talking with the bankers in our group, we learned not only that we shouldn't be intimidated in applying for loans and that we *should* shop for the best deal, but we also found out a little about what bankers are looking for from us and what they expect us to look for from them. "The main thing you need when you go to the bank is a financial statement. You need a profit/loss and cash flow statement. You need to show performance. You need to know where you are going, so you can tell people and make them understand. If you don't have an equity position, the bank probably won't be interested in you unless you have a strong cosigner or a great deal of collateral." "Lenders feel better if you have put a good amount of your own money into the venture. If you don't believe in your business enough to risk your money, why should the bank?"

One of the women in our group, who is a bank president, said, "With old customers I have a track record to look at. I don't ask for a five-year plan, because I know what they can do. I know they already have a plan." "When a bank asks for a five-year or a three-year projection, it's more a demonstration of your management capabilities than tying you down to any specific game plan. Your ability to build a reasonable scenario proves to the banker that you know the business and where potentially it can go, and that you have the acumen to develop an assumption that makes some sense. The business plan is not intended to be used as a report card to see whether you pass or fail." "It is amazing how many loan applicants fill out pro formas showing that they don't anticipate any raises in salaries, or that they must expect their electric bills to go down." "Most of my customers are going to pay a little bit more because my time is worth more and I am going to give them more advice. They are not going to shop for a two-year junior executive and maybe take two points less than I'll charge them. If you aren't comfortable with your banker, just go on up the ladder. Do you think you'll step on toes? So what? It's *your* business, you are important, and it's important to you. You have to do what makes you feel good. When you're trying to get money that makes the difference between the success and failure of your business, don't worry about hurting the banker's feelings."

A woman in our group, a CPA here in Austin, discussed in her client newsletter the problems of getting a loan in a tough financial market. Several of her points bear repeating here. "The loans [a banker] will consider making are the loans that appear to have the least risk. A banker now looks for strong business cash flows that indicate you can repay the debt. . . . A loan officer will look for collateral that can be liquidated if your loan fails. In today's market, many loan officers do not consider real estate to be acceptable collateral . . . . If your business has a good credit record, the banker is more likely to consider your request. The banker will look for accurate, timely financial statements and reports . . . financial and cash flow projections are also very important." [11]

An article in the November 1985 *Ladies' Home Journal* makes another important point about bank loans. Bankers often are unwilling to provide start-up capital for a new business. They are more willing to provide working capital to an entrepreneur who has started a business with financing from personal sources. The article summarizes what should be included in a business plan presented to the bank when applying for a loan:

- How much you want to borrow.
- Concrete projections of both expenses and income.
- How much money you already have.
- Breakdown of exact purposes the borrowed money will be used for.
- The market for your product.
- Who your customers are.
- A list of your business strengths (for example, previous work experience for another business in the same industry).
- What your competition is.

A banker in the group talked about a business plan in terms of the four basic areas that should be addressed thoroughly: finance, marketing, operations, and administration/management. A good business plan doesn't have to be long or complicated. In fact, it should be concise, answering the following questions in as straightforward a manner as possible.

1. What is the basic idea?
2. Who are *you* (the principal), and on what basis (including resume and background) do you think you can implement the idea?
3. Who else is required to achieve the objective stated?
4. How do you plan to develop the market, and what will the ultimate numbers look like?

A brief executive summary should be included to highlight the strengths of the business plan. Critical information for this section includes:

1. The purpose of the business plan, that is, to raise capital.
2. A brief description of the product or service.
3. An outline of the market size and a description of the segment you plan to enter.
4. Product development milestones.

5. A summary of key financial ratios, milestones, and projected income flows.
6. An estimate of the amount of capital the firm requires and the uses to which the desired funds will be put.
7. A brief description of the management team and their experience in the fields where they will work.

A well-written executive summary can sometimes be used as a first step, before presenting the full plan to a potential lender or investor, since it gives enough information to allow a preliminary assessment.[12]

An excellent article in the November 1985 issue of *Ms.* magazine suggests that the physical appearance of the business plan — "a first class typing job" prepared on a word processor for easy updating, and printed out on high-quality paper — should not be overlooked. This article makes an excellent case for *all* entrepreneurs to prepare business plans early, because they force the new entrepreneur to confront problems before they arise. It provides sound advice on a variety of topics, including a list of resources for entrepreneurs.[13]

Taking out a Small Business Administration loan

One form of financing is the so-called SBA loan. (In fact, the Small Business Administration, or SBA, does not actually *make* loans, but rather guarantees a bank 90 percent of the face amount of a loan made by the bank.) Most of our members who have had any experience with such loans tend to think of them as a last resort, but some of the bankers in the group believe SBA loans are often a good option. "This is a government-backed loan. If you don't have a good track record, or collateral, and if you're really willing to give up a whole lot of time and assets, then you go in business with the government. Basically the government owns you." "They'll guarantee your loan up to 90 percent, but they'll take every asset you have." "SBA is a good way to go if you want to do all the paperwork. It is much easier for minorities, such as women. I encourage a lot of people to do it, but it does tie up your assets." "If you feel you really are going to be successful, it's a way to get started, even though you are partners with the government. You don't actually give up a part of your business. It is 100 percent yours once you pay off the loan and the government is off the hook as your guarantor." "They may own you body and soul while their money is at risk, but once you pay it back, the business is *all* yours. With any other investor, you never have that opportunity. Once an investor steps in, you've given up part of your business. If your goal is to own your business totally at the end, the SBA is well worth your consideration."

Not every business qualifies for SBA assistance. "I once made an inquiry about an SBA loan and I could not get one because I deal with editorial matter. That is a First Amendment issue, and the government is not allowed to support anything that takes an editorial position." "SBA loans cannot be made to radio stations, newspapers, or any business of that kind." "Bankers have the option of going in with an applicant on an SBA loan. If the equity position is not there, but the people situation is, and this is the only way to accomplish what she needs to do, I advise her to go the SBA route. I would not make an SBA loan, or *any* loan, if I didn't feel the payback was there." "The SBA doesn't go into the risk-taking business. They have to be pretty sure of the product or service."

Seeking risk capital: private investors

When we talked about creative financing, we explored one of the most interesting avenues open to the entrepreneur: risk capital. Banks don't take risks, and neither does the government. There are, however, many private investors who are interested in making money available to entrepreneurs — at a cost. Money from banks, the government, insurance companies, and finance companies is *debt financing*. You borrow money, and you repay the loan with interest. Money from a private investor represents *equity financing*. The investor provides you money in exchange for a percentage of ownership in your business and future profits.

A private investor — the current "buzzword" for such investors is *venture capitalists* — will want to participate to some degree in the management and policy decisions of your company. This investor will almost certainly want to sit on your board of directors, and will want to find out for herself or himself what problems are, or may soon be, plaguing your company. To protect the investment in your company, as a director he or she will probably be persistent in questioning and probing to find out what's *really* going on, and may even help you spot potential problems that may have been overlooked in a period of rapid growth. A really creative investor can help you appreciate the art of good management. A company cannot succeed, no matter how original and brilliant the idea behind its product or service, until that idea has been brought to fruition through an innovative manager. Such a manager can help you recognize your own strengths and weaknesses, and can help you implement tough changes that can ease cash flow problems: get rid of "losers," whether product lines, services, or people; focus on the "winners," again, whether products, services, or people; strengthen accounting and financial systems; implement a monitoring system to keep you on top of all operations; and, perhaps most important, help create incentives to keep your best people motivated. If management is one of your strengths, a creative investor can help you enhance it. If you are more of an idea person, with little interest in active management, the right investor can make all the difference in the success of your business.

Basically, there are two kinds of private investors: the *active investor* and the *passive investor*. Why would an entrepreneur choose to approach one or the other?

"If you're an entrepreneur who really wants to run your own show, and if you know what you are doing and are a good manager, then you want to get involved with a passive investor. As an entrepreneur, you really have to be more convincing to a passive investor — showing the proprietary nature of your project, the means of protecting your investor, the quality of your business plan, and a myriad of other features of your project. But with a passive investor you might get to keep more of your equity. It depends on your skill and care in negotiating. The active investor might be willing to contribute more resources in terms of accounting, legal, management, etc., and is probably going to cost the entrepreneur more equity than the passive investor." "Many times an entrepreneur is an inventor, a product person, a creative person, but absolutely falls down when it comes to management. The entrepreneur may be the ideal person to start a business, but not to run it. The smart entrepreneur is the one who realizes this weakness and looks for an active investor. For that type of entrepreneur, the best investor is the one who can give the best management help. A terrific partnership to have is a creative person who recognizes that he or she needs somebody good at management, and an innovative manager who appreciates the entrepreneur's creativity."

A private investor will want a business plan, just as a prospective lender will. Venture capitalists interested in fast-growth companies are especially concerned about the quality of the management team. The rule of thumb sometimes quoted is that a venture capitalist would rather have a first-rate management team with a second-rate idea than a first-rate idea with a second-rate management team. The point here is that venture capitalists are usually investing in 10 to 15 companies, and simply don't have the time to ride herd on management in every one of those companies in order to protect their investments.[14]

THE DANGERS OF OUTSIDE FINANCING

As we explored the various avenues for securing working capital, we encouraged our members to share their personal experiences. Not all of these were positive. We were treated to some horror stories, and we learned some of the pitfalls awaiting the unwary entrepreneur who is eager to put her fabulous idea into practice with the help of outside financing. We discovered that an entrepreneur can easily find herself losing not only the control of her business, but also all the time, money, and effort she has invested in building it. Through fear of failure — or of not getting started at all — she can give away too much.

We also learned that entrepreneurs who do not fully understand all the nuances of an investment deal can take advantage of an investor in several ways. They can overinflate the value of their own ideas and their own importance to the company, and they can demand an excessive percentage of the potential profits. They can expose the investor to substantial expense in legal fees, plus the time and effort of exploring and setting up a relationship, and then decide to go elsewhere for funding — leaving the investor with nothing to show for the time and money spent. They can be unrealistic in estimating both potential profits and risks, and they can fail to disclose essential facts that the investor needs to make a sound decision. By focusing too intently on their own priorities, in essence by being greedy, entrepreneurs can abuse prospective financial backers and can cut themselves off from future funding and support. Just as entrepreneurs should guard against giving away too much, so must investors guard against contributing but getting no return or one that is inadequate to the risk.

While entrepreneurs may be extremely creative, and may bring exciting and innovative ideas to the table, still they are asking investors to tie up a large amount of money, at considerable risk, for an indefinite period of time. Investors are necessarily very sensitive to their ROIs (returns on investment). In any negotiation involving venture capital, the greatest difficulties arise in trying to reach an equitable balance between entrepreneur and investor — where one doesn't demand too much or the other not give enough. An equitable balance occurs when the entrepreneur requests a fair amount of capital and when the investor provides enough capital to ensure success. Negotiating an equitable deal for all parties concerned is one of the most delicate and creative accomplishments in the business world!

In seeking outside funding, it is incredibly important to know what you have to offer, what you need, and what you are willing and able to give up in order to get what you want. In putting together a business plan, all of these points should be covered. It is equally as important to consider the investor: what are his or her needs, what are the potential gains he or she may expect, and what will be demanded of the entrepreneur in return for financial aid? How active a role will the investor take in day-to-day management and in strategic decisions? How often, and in what fashion, will the entrepreneur and the investor communicate? What are the expectations of the entrepreneur and the investor for the business — for its growth and possible expansion into new markets? Are they in consonance? What are the performance criteria the investor expects the entrepreneur to meet, and how will they be assessed? At what point will the investor take a hand if these criteria are not met? If the business exceeds expectations, what will the relationship be between investor and entrepreneur?

Speaking from her vantage point as an investor, one woman in our group told us that, consciously or unconsciously, she and most other investors always keep a simple formula in mind when assessing a business proposition: "people + product = payoff." If she can't see the "three *p*'s" in a particular deal, she'll shop around until she finds them.

Negotiation is the key to a successful relationship when outside funding is involved. Both parties—the entrepreneur and the investor—must realize up front who is getting what and at what price.

There are pitfalls when a financial vulture or a greedy entrepreneur wants too much. This is a time when a trusted friend, a good accountant, and an excellent attorney can help immeasurably. One of our members, who is a financier, offers some wise advice: "It's better to have 49 percent of something than 51 percent of nothing." This is a difficult concept for a new entrepreneur to assimilate. In her enthusiasm she can be totally unrealistic. Good negotiating skills and good professional advice are essential to making the best deal for all concerned.

---

[11]*Client Update,* Mary Bird Bowman & Company, Certified Public Accountants (Austin: June 1988)

[12]George Kozmmetsky et al., *Financing and Managing Fast-Growth Companies: The Venture Capital Process* (Lexington, Mass: Lexington Books, 1985)

[13]Emily Card, "The Business Plan: Why No Entrepreneur Should Be Without One," *Ms.* (November 1985)

[14]Michael Gill, (from a transcript of a seminar at the IC Institute, The University of Texas at Austin, April 1985).

Dealing with Risks

How Can I Protect Myself and Others?

PUT IT IN WRITING

The beginning of a new business is the most critical time for the new entrepreneur to work with two first-rate professionals — a lawyer and an accountant — to protect her interests. Dispassionate advice from a seasoned professional can save many times the amount it costs. This is even more true when the new business involves others: a partner, employees, and especially an investor. One critical area in which the entrepreneur needs advice from a lawyer and an accountant is in determining the appropriate structure for the new business venture. Should it be a sole proprietorship, a partnership, or a corporation? What are the advantages or disadvantages of each structure in the particular situation?

As we've suggested earlier, with a family business it is particularly critical that everything be in writing, especially on such sensitive questions as successorship in the event of the death or disability of one of the family members who heads the business. A business can easily go down the tubes while relatives quarrel over who succeeds whom. Family harmony and the success of the business depend on having such issues clearly spelled out in writing, and reviewed by a competent lawyer or accountant, *before* any questions arise. One WIM member advises, based on her own experience, "Don't leave *anything* open-ended!"

One of our members, a lawyer, gave us some pointers on what she calls "critical symptoms" of when you need to consult a lawyer. She says to be on guard against the following:

1. A document that uses language that is ambiguous, incomplete, vague, or that leaves key terms undefined.
2. A situation in which you find it difficult to get precise answers to your questions.
3. A situation where the other side adds or changes terms after you thought you had a deal.
4. A document that contains one-sided or all-or-nothing provisions.
5. A document that is poorly organized or difficult to follow.
6. A unique circumstance for which there are no references or precedents.
7. A situation in which you are being railroaded, where you're given no time to consider the deal or to consult advisors.
8. A situation where you hear big promises, or where someone is making commitments that another party has to keep.
9. A deal that is complex or tied to other arrangements, where your deal is tied to others.

She says a well-prepared document contains the following elements:

1. It has clarity of language, completeness, and understandability.
2. It is well organized and easy to follow.
3. It is fair.
4. It contains standards for the quality of work to be done.
5. It outlines duties: who does what and when.
6. It provides for testing and acceptance.
7. It has clear payment terms: how much and when.
8. It has remedies for partial- and non-performance.
9. It contains procedures for resolving disputes.
10. It has termination clauses: when and how.

Finally, she says you should call a lawyer for the following reasons:

1. For education and to review forms and checklists for routine business.

2. To ensure completeness and discuss "hardstops."
3. To develop strategy for the structure of a deal.
4. When the other side is playing games.
5. If you suspect a setup.
6. At the first sign of serious trouble, foot-dragging, or changing promises.
7. To convey seriousness to the other party.
8. Before threatening suit or taking any action that has legal consequences.
9. When you hear from someone else's attorney.
10. When the other side requests major modifications to a deal.

Selecting professional advisors

"All right," some of our women say, "but where do you find the lawyer or accountant who will understand what you want to do and protect your interests? How do you find the professional advisor who is right for you? And how do you stretch your already limited start-up capital to cover professional fees?" It isn't always easy, but lawyers and accountants in our group have made suggestions about what we should look for, how we should proceed, and how we can get the advice we need while staying on budget.

In looking for any professional advisor, the first (and often best) source of information is friends, relatives, and business acquaintances who are or have been in a similar situation. Who is recommended as smart, honest, easy to work with, and knowledgeable in the area of small businesses, especially start-up businesses? Other people who might advise us are a banker, an insurance agent, or a real estate broker, if these are people whose opinions we value.

Here is some advice from lawyers in our group. As a first step in selecting a lawyer, check with the State Bar Association to find out if there is a specialty section relating to your field. If your business is in an area where there is special certification (e.g., real estate, family law), you might look at the Yellow Pages for specialists listed. Be aware that you'll pay more for the services of a certified specialist who has taken a test in that specialty, and has been in practice for a certain number of years. Other general areas for exploration are the lawyer's contacts at the community, state, and national levels: is he or she positioned to do your business some good through other clients or contacts? Will his or her reputation lend your business credibility?

When you've narrowed your selection to one or a few names, you should call for an appointment to meet your initial choice and talk with him or her about specifics. First, explain who you are, where you are in terms of your business, and where you want to go. It's important for the lawyer to be knowledgeable in the particular areas relevant to your business, and it's also important that he or she be open-minded and receptive to new ideas and approaches. Tell the lawyer what you think you need in the way of legal help. Then see how the lawyer responds to you and your situation. Your gut instinct is a good guide here. Do you like his or her approach? Does the answer seem to fit with your ideas and style? Ask how much direct experience the lawyer has in your field, for example, the computer industry, retail, or real estate.

Lawyers work in two ways: some restrict their advice to legal questions, others give general business guidance. Which do you prefer? If you want help on business strategy, is the lawyer comfortable giving it and is the advice any good? You might want to test this. Some lawyers want to "run the whole show," and don't want the client's active participation. If you want to take an active role, and if you feel it is important to direct the lawyer about the special ins and outs of your own business, you should determine at the outset whether you are working with someone who will respond well to you. Rapport with the lawyer is not the only criterion for a successful working relationship, but it *is* important.

Here are some specific questions to ask.

1. In which areas do you specialize, and what types of clients do you prefer?
2. What do you like about working for businesses like mine, or in my industry?
3. What is the most important piece of advice you could give to someone in my position?
4. What is the biggest mistake a person in my position can make?

5. What is the most common mistake people in my position do make?
6. Are there ways I can use your legal service to prevent problems? If so, how?
7. What is your preferred method of giving information or advice?
8. What is your average turnaround time? How long will it take you to get back to me with an answer when I call with a problem or question?
9. If I were to have legal requirements outside your firm's expertise, how would you handle that? (Our lawyers say beware of anyone who claims to be knowledgeable in every area of the law.)
10. My new business will require multiple legal services. How would you establish priorities in my needs in order to stay within my budget?

Some of our experienced members suggest that "you can save a lot of money if you know how to *use* your lawyer." They suggest working out as much of your deal as possible with the other party in a preliminary, nonbinding format. Then take the detailed information to your lawyer when most of the preparatory work has already been done. He or she can give you a legal analysis, and eliminate loopholes or conflicts, but this will be a much less expensive process than having the lawyer do everything from scratch. Our members also advise that "as much as possible, the clients should deal with the business points and the lawyers should deal with the legal points."

Our lawyers all agree: discuss money up front. Retainer amounts may differ. The lawyer will probably give you a range within which professional fees for services you require should fall. Determine payment terms. Work out a series of progress payments so that you can determine where you are in relation to your budget. Arrange for the lawyer to warn you if you're getting into trouble by running up fees in excess of your budget. If you are considering litigation, try to determine at the outset the merit of a particular case; it may not be worth your investment in legal help. Work out in your own mind what it is you really want the lawyer to do or to tell you. One of our attorneys says, "The more specific you can be about what you want, the more likely it is that you will get what you want for a reasonable fee." Finally, if you're uncomfortable with answers to any of the suggested questions, if you don't like the lawyer's approach, if the fee schedule is beyond your means, continue shopping. It is essential that you choose a legal advisor with whom you can work closely and comfortably.

Our accountants offer similar advice: select candidates among accountants who have been recommended by friends and business acquaintances, and then interview them. First, you will probably be best served by selecting a Certified Public Accountant because he or she will be technically qualified over a broad range of subjects. One who is affiliated with the state or local accounting society, or the American Institute of CPAs, is demonstrating a commitment to the profession and is probably staying current with continuing education in the profession. As with an attorney, the personal rapport you feel with the accountant is important. Ask a few technical questions to determine for yourself how the accountant explains difficult concepts. You will be working closely with this individual on matters crucial to the success of your business, and you must understand fully both the general concepts being presented and the specifics that relate to your daily operations. It's important that he or she communicates clearly at a level you understand; an accountant who wants to impress you with superior technical knowledge and specialized language is not a good bet.

When you interview a prospective accountant, ask what experience he or she has with businesses of the same size as yours and in the same or related fields. A firm specializing in multinational corporations would probably not be the best choice for advising you on your new venture. You might want to ask for names of clients you can talk with who are in businesses similar to yours. (This will take a few days, since the accountant must get permission from clients to use their names.) As with an attorney, it's a good idea to find out what contacts the prospective accountant has. Accountants can be an excellent source of leads on bankers, lawyers, vendors, and other people of importance to a new entrepreneur.

Determine the services you will require. The accountant

should be willing to provide you with weekly or bimonthly cash flow projections, at least in the early stages of your business, so that you can anticipate and possibly stave off a cash crunch. He or she should also provide monthly profit and loss statements to help you gauge your performance. The accountant should be able to help you file for your federal and state tax I.D. numbers, and should be knowledgeable about out-of-state sales taxes. If you're dealing with a large firm, be sure that you meet and talk with the accountants who will actually be assigned to your business. Find out what services the individual accountant or firm provides beyond auditing and tax functions. These could include financial planning, advice on management and on personnel matters, and system planning. Even though you might not need these services immediately, they might be helpful as your business grows. You should also see if the accountant provides any client aids that might be helpful to a small business. These could include a business guide, advice on selecting computer systems, newsletters on use of computer software for maintaining records, or special assistance in setting up monthly financial statements.

Again, our accountant members advise that fees be discussed at the outset. Don't be afraid to negotiate rates: accountants always have a fee schedule that is negotiable. Settle on a schedule that is affordable, or you may have a bad shock when the first bill arrives.

Fools rush in, you shouldn't

As some of our women have learned from personal experience, no matter how eager she is to get started, the most important time for the entrepreneur to go slowly and easily is at the negotiating table with the prospective investor. *Everything* must be clearly understood by both parties *and it must be in writing,* with all the *i*'s dotted and the *t*'s crossed. This is the time when the new entrepreneur, especially, needs a professional support group to give her counsel, because this is when the whole deal can start to fall apart. One woman, an investor, said, "I can't say it often enough. It's at the beginning that both of you must protect yourselves through clear understanding and written documents. If the deal — who's giving what and in exchange for what — isn't absolutely understood by both parties at the outset, the whole thing can go sour very quickly, and it usually can't be put back together after that."

When outside investment is concerned, it is essential to explore all sorts of questions regarding control, reporting, and planned expansions, and to resolve the questions to the satisfaction of both parties before any deal is consummated. Again, it is imperative to *put the agreement in writing*. No matter how cordial the relationship between entrepreneur and investor, the arrangement between them should not be on an informal "hand shake" basis. This rule is just as essential — or perhaps even more so — when the entrepreneur and investor are close friends or even members of the same family as when they are merely acquaintances who have come together over a business arrangement. "Business is business and friendship is friendship. Don't assume that the person you are dealing with, regardless of gender, is going to treat you as a friend." If things go badly — or even very well — there can suddenly be a disagreement about terms or about the respective roles of the two parties, and either or both can suffer unnecessarily. The expense of consulting a lawyer to help define details of an agreement is a small one compared with the expense of litigation to resolve a conflict after the fact.

While this advice seems so obvious as to be a cliche, we found in our own group that it is often ignored in the excitement of putting a deal together, or just because the other party seems to be "such a good guy." "We were just so flattered, so bowled over, that someone would take our idea and put hard cash behind it," one entrepreneur explained about a deal that had gone very sour. "Our guard was down." "We were very impatient," another explained. "Going the bank route would have taken six to eight months, and we were ready to go *then*. This fellow came along and said he could get us started right away. We asked, kind of timidly, if we could have something in writing, but he always said, 'Hey, this is a small company, there are just the three of us,' and we went for it. The next thing we knew he was paying some of his other business expenses out of the profits we had earmarked for expansion, and we found out we couldn't do a thing about it."

Trust your instincts

It was all summed up for us by one of our entrepreneurs who learned her lesson the hard way. "Don't let the fact that somebody has taken an interest in you affect your good judgment. Shop and negotiate to get the best deal from an investor; be sure you really know what he or she has to offer. Have an independent attorney who can negotiate your position. Make sure from a legal standpoint that everything is documented and in order as you want it to be. Establish and pursue good business procedures and protocol in terms of board meetings and minutes. Don't let your guard down when you're dealing with family or friends, or anyone you know. Finally, listen to your gut feeling. If you have reservations about the person or the deal, don't go for it."

One point that came across loud and clear: entrepreneurs can get into trouble because of honest misunderstandings, but they can also be taken by investors who deliberately take advantage of their need and their naivete. Financial vulturism is alive and well in our country today. Unfortunately, women and minorities are the ones who are most vulnerable to it, because we are still the "new kids on the block" when it comes to starting businesses. Organizations for women and other minorities are springing up around the country to help us help each other. Another new source of help are magazines directed specifically to the needs of women in business. We women sometimes allow ourselves to be intimidated by male investors because they are "businessmen," and we feel they understand business practices better than we do. We've got to look beyond that stereotype and see what this person is really offering us. As newcomers to the entrepreneurial world, it's especially important for us to learn to differentiate between the vultures and the creative and responsible investors who can be instrumental in helping a new business grow and flourish for the benefit of both parties. In learning to make this distinction, it is essential for a woman to pay attention to her instinct or gut feelings. This "intuition" we possess is really a culturally nurtured survival mechanism; it's common sense honed by years of protecting ourselves. When we listen to it, we seldom let ourselves get hurt!

One of our women, the founder and co-owner of a computer company in Austin, is going through a difficult period with her company. She and her partners were looking for new venture capital and were approached by a prospective investor. Happily, they recognized his offer for what it was, and realized they were dealing with a financial vulture in time to turn him down and start taking defensive measures. "We spent a considerable amount of time this past year developing a business plan on a growth strategy. At the same time the president of the company and I were fighting off a takeover strategy by a larger company that could have put us out of business. It took us three and a half months to turn that around. We've had a tough year, but we've come through this far, and we're going to keep at it."

WHAT HAPPENS IF I FAIL?

Not all entrepreneurs succeed. Lots of new businesses don't make it. In fact, one of our members reported reading that eight out of ten businesses fail in the first five years, and one out of three in the first ten years. Fifty-three percent of all business failures and bankruptcies occur in the first five years of a new firm's life. Nearly 30 percent fail in years six through ten, and the remaining 70 percent of failures occur in firms in existence more than ten years.[15] What happens to entrepreneurs whose businesses have failed? If failure happens to us, then what? A lot of failures stem from inadequate planning — entrepreneurial risk taking carried to its extreme. "They just tromp right out there, can't meet their cash flow, and they don't worry about it." Others, as we've seen, fail because of undercapitalization, or from growth that is too rapid for the new company to absorb and manage. Many fail because of poor management; the skills that are required to start a new business are not those required to manage it effectively. The absence of managerial skills need not lead to failure. As we've seen from members of our own group, one of whom is described in a preceding chapter, if an entrepreneur recognizes that her skills are appropriate to starting a business, rather than running one, she can always get out and start another business and let a competent manager take over once each new business is on its feet. Self-awareness is a strength that more than compensates for the weakness in managerial talent.

Is failure the end of the world?

In our group we have the sense that it is more difficult for women to face failure than it is for men. We take failure personally. If we fail in business, we truly believe this is a reflection on our character. We must, somehow, be bad people. We are ashamed. Where a man will go through bankruptcy, talk about it, and immediately get started on something new, bankruptcy would cast an awful shadow over a woman's entire life.

A young woman who is active in our group became an entrepreneur at an incredibly early age, achieved success and substantial acclaim as a magazine publisher, led her business in a tremendous growth spurt, and then watched it fail by the time she was 21. Her experience of failure, while certainly unusual in terms of her age, is fairly typical of the emotional trauma it can create for a woman. "When the business went down, I felt like I had disappointed everybody and that I was worthless. It was *my* guilt. My whole life felt like it was crumbling. I lost my marriage, I was alone with a two-year-old daughter. I felt that I had lost the respect of all my peers and all my friends. I felt like I deserved whatever I got because I had failed in business. I thought about not working at all and just raising children."

For many of us failure is not just a social stigma, it's a potential financial disaster. Increasingly, we women find ourselves as single parents and sole breadwinners for our children. When we have sole responsibility for raising our children do we dare take risks? Men do. Is it different for us?

One thing we agreed is that a woman must go into a high-risk situation with her eyes wide open. She has to consider the possibility of failure, and decide if she can handle it and how. "You have to be able to look at it and say 'What is the downside of the business? What's the worst that could happen to me?'"

"I recently attended a management seminar, listening to a bunch of very successful business people, mostly men. They said over and over again, 'Don't be afraid of failure. We learn more from failing than from succeeding.' I've always had a tremendous fear of failing, but since hearing those people talk about their own failures and how they've learned from them, I've tried to be more of a risk taker." "I had never worked, and when I took over the company after my husband died, I kept remembering one thing he told me many times over the years: Always think of the worst thing that can happen and base your decision on that. Sometimes a problem is terrifying, but in the long run, it is not really as bad as we think." "I remember my mother telling me, 'It's not how many times you fall that counts; it's how many times you pick yourself up.' " "You have to learn how to take your knocks and keep coming back."

When our young friend shared with us the story of her own business failure, it had a gratifying conclusion: the way she bounced back. "I went into 'seclusion' for three years, working for another company. In that time I grossed about half a million dollars worth of business for them, which made me feel I wasn't so bad after all. If I could have seen that three years ago, I could have gotten on with things a lot sooner. I doubt that a man would take so long to regain his self-esteem. I think the recovery time would be more like 15 minutes." But she *did* recover and now, at 24, is starting another new publishing business—but with a far greater understanding of the importance of financial controls, and with the firm idea of planned growth tied to financial performance.

One of the most successful entrepreneurs in the group described to us the blackest days early in the life of her business. "I had been in business three or four years the first time I faced the possibility that I might go under. This is a very real moment in most small businesses. There are points where you are growing so rapidly that to make a mistake could have colossal financial ramifications. The first time I faced that possibility, I sat down and thought that the worst thing that could happen to me at that point was to lose my own duplicating shops and get a job as a sales rep for one of the suppliers from whom I had been buying. I felt that I could, indeed, go back to work for somebody else. Once I realized that, and dealt with my worst fear, then I could move forward again. If you don't face it and deal with it, your fear can paralyze you."

Perhaps one reason why women entrepreneurs have a lower failure rate than their male counterparts is that women tend to generate alternatives. The fear they feel and face produces enough adrenaline to stimulate their creative energies. If the business isn't working in this one direction, perhaps veering a little into a new market, or a slightly modified product line, or an expanded array of services will make it go. The pragmatism that most women have learned from childhood stands them in good stead when it comes to adjusting dreams to fit financial realities!

In facing up to and dealing with our fears, we must also be unflinchingly realistic about our chances of success. The young woman who described the failure of her fast-growing publishing business gave us some insights. She told us about her realization, in retrospect, that she let her business continue far too long after it was in trouble. "I wish I had stopped everything that I was doing and corrected the problems, but people kept assuring me I was about to turn the corner. Then I was always pressed to get the next issue out. I would think, 'What will the public think? What is going to happen if I stop right now?' My ego was in this. Everybody was watching me. I felt that I had to keep going and make up the difference somewhere. That was the worst decision I could make." Others in the group who have also experienced business failure agreed. "It is hard to know when to quit." "One of the things you have to know, as your business takes off, is where to *stop* to preserve your success." "You tend to think more is better. That's not always the case."

The upside of failure

Women must overcome their cultural hang-up on the idea that failure is a terminal disease. One of the most exciting contributions we have made as a group is to convince one another that women are allowed to fail. Failure should be considered as just another learning situation, a growth experience that offers a challenge. The ability to accept — and to learn from — failure is especially important to anyone starting her own business. "The successful entrepreneur is able to view failure as a learning experience. He or she says, 'I won't make that same mistake again, and I'll move on from here.' "

Women who had survived failure had an important observation to make. "A lot of those failures are almost a stepping stone toward ultimate success because you learn so much. If you experience it, then you *know*."

"We feel confident this time throwing everything we have into the business because we did it once and we can do it again. This time we can do it better, because we're starting with all that education and hindsight behind us." "Winning entails taking a risk, putting yourself on the line. It requires having the courage of your convictions. You won't win if you don't get in and do everything you can to reach your goal." "If you don't risk, you can't make changes in your life."

------

[15] Donald L. Sexton and Raymond W. Smilor, *The Art and Science of Entrepreneurship* (Cambridge, Mass.: Ballinger Publishing Co., 1986).

Getting Started
What Do I Do First?

HOW DO I MAKE THE MOST OF MY PRESENT CONTACTS?
It takes a lot of courage and a lot of drive to examine all the
challenges facing a prospective entrepreneur and still decide to
go ahead. In our group we try to be realistic, if not brutal, in
examining the downside: the hard work, the long hours, and
the interruptions to family and social life; the difficulties of getting financing; the dangers associated with outside financing;
and the ever-present risk of failure. After considering all the
negatives, many of us feel undaunted. We still want our own
businesses. We want to be our own bosses. We want to make
the decisions and take the consequences. We want the glory —
or the gloom. We want to be entrepreneurs!

What next? How does a woman get started with her own
business? What resources can she tap to help her get the new
business off the ground? Where should she turn to get a head
start? What and who does she know that can make a difference
in the critical early stages? What must she do to make her business go, and how long should she be prepared to stay afloat before the business begins to make her a living?

Who do I know?
First of all, in any retail or service business, it's essential to get
the word out. Somehow the new entrepreneur must get the

customers or the clients in the door. The easiest place to start is with the people she already knows personally, socially, or through business or community contacts. This usually includes a broad range of people, starting with: immediate family and their business and social contacts; other family members; friends; neighbors; her own previous employers and, if she's married, her husband's employer and other professional contacts; the law firm and accountants that represent her in her business negotiations; her physicians; acquaintances from college days; members of social and community organizations in which she's been active; PTA members, if she has children in school; members of tennis, golf, or exercise clubs she's joined; business people, vendors, service people, and media representatives she's contacted through her previous employment or through volunteer work; and real estate agents, bankers, appraisers, and stock brokers with whom she has had dealings.

When she's starting out in business, the new entrepreneur will find it useful to actually list the various contacts she can approach. Then it's a good idea to step back and assess the list, ranking the people on it according to what they can be counted on to do that will help her get started. This is one of the times when a woman can call on everyone in her network. The more active she has been in maintaining her contacts, in offering help and advice, and in being there for other women, the more help she can expect now in establishing her new business. (See Chapter 6.)

In discussing this approach, our group made the point that while a few of the new entrepreneur's contacts will definitely be behind her all the way, hoping for and willing to make an effort toward her success, an equal number may actually be antagonistic toward her personally or toward the idea of her business. Far more of her contacts will be indifferent; they simply won't care if she starts a business or if that business succeeds or fails. Less straightforward than who likes the entrepreneur herself and who doesn't is the separate question of who likes her *business:* some of those who actually love her, may, for one reason or another, either dislike the idea of her business or otherwise feel unable to support it. Conversely, there will probably be some who admire the entrepreneur's abilities, although they don't like her at all; they may not want to see her socially, but think well enough of her skills to recommend or even use her services, and they can be a real asset in building her new business.

Before making any attempt to call on her contacts for help, it is important for the entrepreneur to analyze these relationships and to categorize people according to their interest in her, their probable reactions to her new business, and their willingness to help her get started. For example, while she can safely assume that her family loves her, they may consciously or unconsciously oppose her desire to start a business because of concern for her welfare, because they are reluctant to be deprived of her company, or because they fear the additional work load that will fall on them when she is spending most of her waking hours trying to get her business going.

Friends have even more potential conflicts than family when it comes to the entrepreneur's new business. Some may see themselves losing a regular tennis or bridge partner, or a babysitting co-op mate. Others may see more carpooling in their own futures if she's not around to do her share. Those who are already in business may see her as a potential competitor or may resent her for "getting ahead." Some may want to protect her from taking on too much and exhausting herself. Others may see her move as totally positive and be enthusiastic that she is making a career advance or that she is breaking out of the homemaker mold and realizing her potential as a businesswoman.

It's in the area of acquaintances that the new entrepreneur should concentrate a lot of her thought about the prospects for support of her business. While these people are far more likely to be indifferent to her as a person, they will have fewer personal reasons for opposing her business than will either family or friends. Many of them may support her venture either through their personal need for the goods or services she will provide, or their recognition of her abilities in organizations in which they have served together, or their desire to support women in business. These are the people to whom the entrepreneur can appeal on the basis of the uniqueness of her product or service, or its superiority over the competition. They can be objective in assessing what she proposes to provide, her ability to deliver it, and their own needs, and those of others, for that product or service. If the new entrepreneur can appeal to this group, she may find the support she needs not only in getting started, but in sustaining her business.

Professional advisors

Among the professionals that the new entrepreneur has included in her list of contacts may be some who can give her valuable advice in starting her business. These people — lawyers, accountants, financial advisors, bankers, insurance brokers, realtors — may be close enough to provide some counsel as a favor, but she should select carefully among them and establish early professional relationships with advisors who can be dispassionate about her business and can steer her away from some of the pitfalls that may await her. Here she isn't looking for someone to love her *or* her business, but rather someone to keep her on track. Above all she'll want to avoid those who will do whatever she instructs, without questioning her or pointing out the errors in her thinking. They might be enthusiastic and supportive, but advisors should never let their professional judgments be colored by their enthusiasm.

It is worth noting here that men starting new businesses don't have this additional worry about "who's for or against me." In our society, entrepreneurship is an acceptable role for men, but it still carries many emotional overtones for women. The need to anticipate, and deal with, the attitudes of others toward her new venture is an extra burden for a woman entrepreneur who already faces all the difficulties of getting her business off the ground.

SETTING OBJECTIVES

It is important for the entrepreneur to give some thought to long-range goals for her business as well as to set and meet daily objectives for getting started. Beyond the generalized goal of "success," one woman in our group suggested that the prospective business owner should think in terms of an "ideal day" six years in the future. On that ideal day, what does she see herself doing? How will she be spending her time? How many staff people will she have to help her? Is she meeting the public, or in the back room handling the "nuts and bolts" of her business? Is she gearing up for expansion, or trying to concentrate her efforts on a few blue-chip customers or clients? Is she traveling, or focusing on local business? Her conceptualization of where she wants to be will help her formulate her immediate objectives and shape the future of her business. Even if she changes her long-term plans frequently in the intervening months, she will have a direction to pursue in making her initial contacts and establishing her first working relationships.

At this point, work begins in earnest. To head her business toward the intermediate goal of solvency, as well as the long-range goal she has pictured for herself, she'll have to meet some very basic day-by-day performance objectives. One member of our group suggested that a new business owner should establish a routine of at least 15 specific tasks she should undertake each day to get her business established. These could start with "Meet with Jane and try to get introductions to three of her professional colleagues," or "Attend a Chamber of Commerce luncheon and introduce myself and my new business." Our member called this "reality testing," because if the entrepreneur finds herself unwilling or unable to achieve these goals each day, she's not interested in the realities of launching and developing her business. If she doesn't have the energy to push herself this hard, she'd better choose a career path other than entrepreneurship.

The process

Having decided on her long-term goals, and having set herself some realistic daily objectives to get her business started, the new entrepreneur also needs to establish some guidelines for herself. What present resources can she commit to developing her business? If she needs financial assistance, can she qualify? How will she measure her progress over time and determine whether to continue on her present path or to devise a new approach?

Allocating resources

In any business, resources can be divided into three categories: money, people, and time. What she must do is calculate what she has in each of these categories, and what she can allocate to starting her business. Initially, she probably has no people on whom she can call, other than herself. She may rely on people she can bring in on a contract basis, whose specific skills will complement her own. These people will be available to her only when she needs them to fulfill specific contract obligations. Still, she must locate the talents she will require and have arrangements in place to bring in the necessary support when her work load demands it.

As she starts her business, money will almost certainly be in limited supply. She must assure herself at the outset that she will be adequately funded to do whatever promotion proves necessary to launch her business, to pay free-lance support people as she needs them, to cover production costs until receivables start to come in, and to accommodate either growth spurts or slow periods. To determine her potential expenditures over the first 24 months of her business, and how she will handle them, she should prepare a detailed business plan covering her first two years, with projections extending out to five years. This is a more detailed working document than she would normally have had to prepare for a banker or other financial backer. It should tell her what is required of her personally (beyond "sweat capital") and what she must raise from private sources in addition to the long-range working capital she may be getting from a backer.[16]

In the beginning stages of her business, the entrepreneur will probably find that her greatest resource allocation will be in time — her own. She must be prepared to devote virtually every waking hour to getting her business off the ground. To leverage her time, she must establish strict priorities for her activities. Which will pay off immediately? Which have potentially the best return? Which will produce additional useful contacts? She must concentrate her efforts on high-yield activities. And, of course, she must allocate time, money, and personnel (herself) not only to attracting business but also to providing an outstanding product or service to her early customers or clients.

Charting progress
Our group suggested that a good way for a new business own-

er to monitor her progress is to list her objectives, one to a sheet, and then list specific activities related to achieving each one. She should itemize time, people, and dollars that will be consumed for each of the listed objectives. Along with costs, she should add a time line indicating when each phase should begin and when she should expect to complete it. By planning all this in advance, she can see ahead of time if some objectives are too costly for the results they might yield. She'll also have a time and cost projection against which to measure her progress. These projections will be useful in helping her set initial priorities, and in charting her progress toward achieving her objectives.

At this stage it is especially important for the new entrepreneur to establish a close working relationship with a good accountant who is sensitive to her needs. At no other time is cash flow monitoring as critical as in the beginning stages of a new business. It is essential for her to establish cost controls at the outset, and to know on a monthly basis if she is operating in the red or the black. If her business is in the red, she must stimulate her creative juices and turn the situation around. Recognizing financial danger signs too late can lead to disaster.

Before she actually gets started, the new business owner should give some thought to what might happen when orders start to come in. Aside from advance preparation for free-lancers to provide services needed to fulfill specific contracts, she should think about other services, equipment, and supplies she might need if she's suddenly deluged with business. Will she be able to handle telephone calls, office work, and billings herself, or will she need part- or full-time clerical help? Is her office or manufacturing space adequate? Does she need an additional telephone line? What will expansion do to her cash flow? The problems of sudden unanticipated growth can be every bit as devastating to a new business as can unexpectedly slow growth. The new business owner should be prepared to survive either extreme.

---

[16]Emily Card, "The Business Plan: Why No Entrepreneur Should Be Without One," *Ms.* (November 1985)

TWELVE

Getting Started

How Do I Make It Happen?

WHAT DO I HAVE TO SELL? ME!
The new entrepreneur, or any woman entering the business world, should recognize that the first and most important thing she has to market is herself. This is a tough hurdle for most women starting in business. It is especially difficult for those returning to the business world after several years away from their professional careers. Often, these women have come to define themselves in terms of their roles at home — as wives, mothers, cooks, home-repair specialists, PTA members, and community volunteers — rather than as potentially terrific businesspeople. In our society, women are trained to underplay their assets. Married women, especially, are trained to promote the outstanding virtues of their husbands and children while undervaluing their own. This cultural convention makes it particularly difficult for a woman to think of herself as a marketable commodity.

Whether she's stepping directly out of a corporate role into her own business, or making a business venture her vehicle for returning from a career as a homemaker, a new entrepreneur usually has to change her self-concept before she can begin to market herself and her skills to others. As we have mentioned so frequently, she must somehow develop that overwhelmingly important ingredient of success: self-confidence. The more comfortable and assertive she becomes at "blowing her own horn" with conviction, the sooner she will gain the self-confidence necessary to succeed as an entrepreneur.

Over and over again, women in our group have made the point that whether she is an entrepreneur, a top-level manager, or a professional, what a woman sells first and foremost is herself. Each of us is her own product first, and how we come across to the public is important in achieving our goals. As individuals, we each bring special attributes, experience, needs, and interests to our careers. These special abilities help us to choose our work, and to make a go of it. "I've always been a numbers freak. I never thought in terms of profit. I just thought of making the numbers work." "I was just looking for a good preschool facility for my children, and I couldn't find what I wanted. I started looking around, and it didn't exist. I did my market research, I got my numbers together, and I figured with what I knew — my formal education and my experience — I could make it work. I tell you, it's paid off." "I answered an ad, and they wanted me to do a membership list for them. I said I wasn't interested in working on their membership list, but I did have a degree in journalism, and might be interested in doing a newsletter for them. That was the beginning." Recognizing our special gifts — and our individual personalities — allows us to develop and use them to the fullest in selling ourselves, and therefore advancing our career goals.

Market research

While she is working on herself, adjusting her attitudes and self-conceptions to fit her new role, the new entrepreneur must also find out what it is she has to sell, how, and to whom. She must do some careful market research before she can begin to sell her product or services. Here she can be comfortable drawing on her widest circle of acquaintances, because she isn't asking for help starting her business, she's asking for information: Who's out there in the field? Will my business be unique in the community? If not, what are the greatest strengths of the existing competition? What are their weaknesses? What are the needs of the community that are not served by the products or services now offered?

In assessing both perceived needs and existing competition, the would-be entrepreneur will gain an idea of how to position her own new firm. Unless she is in a very small community, there will probably be other businesses, possibly quite large ones, offering competitive products and services. She must then tailor her own offering to make it stand out. For example, in a service business she might concentrate her efforts on either a specific market segment where she has particular expertise, or on a "boutique" service that can respond quickly to a client's needs and tackle small jobs that might not be lucrative for large firms with high overhead. In assessing what's available, and measuring it against what she proposes to offer, she should come up with a basis for written proposals showing prospective clients what financial or other quantifiable benefits they can expect to realize as a result of dealing with her.

Having identified her natural market and her strongest sales appeal, she should then establish priorities among her potential clients. She should decide who needs her product or service most, who has the greatest ability to pay, and who has the best linkages to her next prospect. In other words, she should position herself to make the most of her first contract.

I'm my most important product

While the entrepreneur analyzes the market and her own competitive edge, she should keep in mind one basic fact of business life: Whatever the product or service she has to offer, what she is ultimately selling is *herself*. When the prospective client is forced to choose between two virtually identical services, what will ultimately tip the scales is the impression made by the individuals offering the services. The person who sells herself (or himself) more effectively will get the business.

Our group decided that one of the most difficult lessons a new entrepreneur — or any other woman in business — must learn is to get out and sell herself and her business. She has to learn to talk about herself and what she does to just about everybody she meets, and she must be positive, enthusiastic, and convincing. For most women, talking business doesn't come naturally. Whether it's chatting in the elevator, or lunching with golf cronies, men seem automatically to talk business. We women (being more interesting people!) have a whole range of subjects to discuss, and business is frequently at the bottom of the list. When we go out into the world to start our own businesses, we must change our priorities and put business on top as a topic of conversation.

Packaging the message

In analyzing who is for, against, or indifferent to her success, the new entrepreneur should have begun to recognize that people typically respond to her and her business because of their own interests, not hers. She should keep that firmly in mind when trying to persuade them of the value of her product or service. She must come up with a message that describes accurately what she feels, thinks, and believes about herself and what she is selling, but a message that is also meaningful to her audience. Her message must be relevant both to herself and to prospective buyers. Good market research will help her achieve this nice balance, by identifying both her own unique capabilities and the unmet needs and interests of her audience.

In an ideal situation, where the new entrepreneur has unlimited funds, it would be best to hire a market research company to assess the prospects for the new business. In a more typical real-world situation, it's the entrepreneur who does her own research. One of our WIM members who wanted to open a retail store, and didn't have the funds to hire a professional market researcher, tackled the project herself. These are some of the questions she explored.

1. Is this the right time to open this type of business?
2. Which types of businesses have the greatest potential for success? Does my specialty retail shop fit into that category?
3. What is my competition in the community? Is the need sufficient to support more than one store of this kind?
4. Does the location I've chosen give me the highest possible visibility and also flexibility for stocking my goods?

When the new entrepreneur must do her own market research, it's useful to bring together a group of experienced people to brainstorm her idea. Having them look at her proposed venture from the perspective of their combined expertise can point up a lot of potential pitfalls. She can then analyze their comments and suggestions and make an intelligent decision about whether she wants to forge ahead.

Once having honed her message, she must start the process of repeating it until it penetrates the consciousness of prospective clients or customers. It must come across in a personal, one-on-one style, even though it may reach members of her audience by telephone, by mail, or through one of the media instead of through a personal contact. The message, in whatever form it's delivered, must always be consistent, keeping to the theme that is clearest and most meaningful to her and to the people she's trying to reach.

PROSPECTING FOR BUSINESS

First the new entrepreneur explores her own contacts and begins to present herself and her business to the community through relationships she has already established. Then she must widen her horizons, making herself and her business known to strangers. Selling never ends! As one of our members commented, "We're always selling, no matter what business or profession we're in. The trick is to find out what people want, how to give it to them, and how to make yourself and them feel good about it."

Several of the women in our group have made their careers in sales or in sales training. They provided useful advice for the new entrepreneur, or any woman in business, about what it takes to sell successfully. One summarized it for us: "There are three elements of selling. One is activity level: doing what's necessary on a daily basis—making telephone calls for appointments, giving presentations, and asking people to buy. The second is skills: having the ability to present, to understand client needs, to close, and to overcome objections. The third is attitude: being able to handle rejection, being a self-starter, being open to new ideas, and being positive. All three are essential to success."

Cold calling

One technique we discussed at length can be particularly important for a new business person, and that is cold calling—establishing potential sales relationships through unsolicited telephone calls. Depending on how this is handled, it can lead to fruitful relationships or it can turn off any future contact. It is a skill that must be learned and practiced in order to become effective. As one woman emphasized, "Successful cold calling is a numbers game. You have to do it *a lot*."

We started our discussion by agreeing that cold calls can be very annoying. Some of our women said they always refuse to talk to people who have not previously written to state their business. Some said their companies routinely refuse to provide names of individuals in key positions, or to put cold callers through to them. Yet most of us agreed that a polite, intelligent sales call often provides information we need, and helps us to make buying decisions.

After discussing the pros and cons of cold calls, what annoys us, and what makes such calls work, we came up with a few hints for making cold calls both palatable and potentially successful. The guidelines were developed by one of our WIM members while she was establishing her own business.

1. Call during a productive time in your day, when you have lots of energy. Don't make cold calling a last resort activity that you fit into a few dead minutes in your schedule.
2. Set aside time every day for calling. Don't put it off.
3. Be aware of time differences in different parts of the country, and also be sensitive to other people's schedules. Don't call when they're just leaving for lunch, or when they're apt to be leaving the office for home. Try to schedule your call to reach them when they're alert and interested in talking to you.
4. Be polite to the operator, receptionist, or secretary who you reach. Tell her or him what you want to talk about, and who (person or position) you hope to reach. This first contact is important; the person who takes your initial call can help you make the necessary contact, or can see to it that your call never gets to the right individual. If you make a friend of that telephone contact, you often can get useful information and a head start on impressing the person who makes the decision about buying.

5. If you can't reach the decision maker, or are referred to an assistant, explain your purpose to that person. The decision maker may have delegated responsibility to him or her and may rely on his or her advice. In any event, by getting that person to listen to you and to understand your position, you have one more friend to help sell for you. (Some of our members felt that a third party couldn't do justice to their sales message, especially on a technical product or service. Still, we all agreed it is better not to turn off any contact by insisting on speaking *only* to someone in authority.)

6. When you reach the person to whom you want to speak, always ask if it's a convenient time to talk. If not, see if you can reschedule your call at a better time. If the person seems reluctant to talk to you at all, ask if you may call back in a few weeks time, or if he or she would prefer to be removed from your call list. If you're asked not to call back at all, respect that wish.

7. Respond to the tone and style of the person to whom you are talking. If he or she is terse and hurried, keep your message brief and specific. If the person's style is warm and friendly, take more time to establish the relationship, and go into greater detail about your product or service.

8. Don't waste your time, or your prospect's. Do some homework before you make your call. Know your product and what you have to offer, and also know something about the company you're calling and the specific benefits of your product or service relative to the company's needs.

9. At the beginning, tell the prospect that you'll take only a specific amount of time. Respect that schedule; complete your presentation within the time you've requested.

10. Have a script that focuses on benefits, and stick to it. Stay in control of the conversation, keeping the emphasis on what you or your product can do for the prospect.

11. Provide personal references or product testimonials to establish your credibility or your product's.

12. Never make the other person wrong.
13. Listen to what the other person says. Respond to the tone and content, and adjust your presentation accordingly.
14. Always give the prospective customer a chance to talk and explain what he or she needs or wants. Build rapport by demonstrating your understanding.
15. If your product or service competes with one the prospect now uses, find out what he or she likes best about your competitor, and what changes and improvements are desired. If you can provide those changes and improvements, explain how.
16. Don't be afraid to ask for the sale. Too many people are unsuccessful at closing because they can't bring themselves to ask.
17. Follow up on your call with a letter restating the benefits you've described. Include a reference or testimonial to increase your credibility.
18. Even if there is no immediate prospect of a sale, leave the door open to call back. And *do* call back.

Keeping clients or customers happy

Our successful women experienced in sales told us that buying is usually a combination of logic and emotion. People want to feel good about their decisions, and someone who is positive and enthusiastic about her product or service can help them feel that way. Usually people respond to warmth, whether it's projected in person or over the telephone. Some of our women were quick to say that they responded more logically than emotionally, and that they found many sales appeals artificially cheerful. They preferred to have sales appeals made on a logical basis, with facts carefully enumerated in writing. They wanted to be left alone to consider the benefits and to make their decisions rationally. We agreed that it is important for any sales professional to be sensitive to these personal styles, and to tailor presentations accordingly, knowing when to back off and send a written proposal outlining the offer, and when to walk the prospect through it, with plenty of opportunity for interaction.

Once the entrepreneur has made a sale or established a client relationship, she must keep that customer or client happy. One important ingredient in ensuring satisfaction is not to overpromise. She must not try to do all things for all people, but should be realistic in assessing what she or her product can do for the prospect, and careful to describe what she has to offer — and no more. She must be sure that the prospect's expectations are in line with what she can deliver. It's a good idea to put the proposal in writing, with cost estimates clearly stated, leaving no room for surprises. In the written proposal, she should outline her understanding of the need or problem, her objective (what she proposes to do or supply), and the estimated cost of the product or service. A brief summary reinforces the point.

In many situations, especially if the deal is complex or unusual, it is a good idea to have a written contract or production agreement spelling out what will be provided and the estimated costs. Sometimes this is not feasible, but it's always essential that the businessperson and the customer or client both have a clear understanding of needs, promises, and prices.

To perform effectively, the businessperson may sometimes have to tell the customer or client that he or she is wrong, that a particular decision or position can be destructive. This is a particularly difficult situation for a woman, who has been culturally conditioned to try to please. One of our WIM members is a consultant who represents clients in the Middle East. She led a discussion in our group dealing with clients who are upset, an attitude that can easily arise when the entrepreneur/consultant must tell the client he or she is wrong. One of her strongest points is that the entrepreneur must be totally honest, with herself and with her client. She must assure herself at the outset of the client's goals and objectives, and she must be satisfied that her service can achieve those goals. She must also be certain the client's expectations do not exceed her ability to deliver. "It is exceedingly important to be very realistic about what your services can do for somebody and what those services involve." The entrepreneur must also realize "you can't please everybody all the time." Some clients must just be written off as what she calls "suicide clients, because they are looking for you to fail before you even start. It justifies *their* failure." Both entrepreneur and client must also recognize that there are forces beyond the control of either—sometimes things go wrong. If she has established an honest, realistic projection of what her services can achieve, and fails to meet that projection, she and the client must face that outcome openly.

On the other side of the coin from pointing out to the client where he or she is wrong is the situation where the entrepreneur herself is wrong. When her mistake in judgment or an incorrect decision might have a negative consequence to the customer or client, it can be uncomfortable for her to admit she's made an error. Still, to maintain her integrity and that of the business relationship, she must acknowledge her mistake. If she has acted honestly, and to the best of her ability, she should be able to say "I was wrong," and still keep the respect of her client or customer. One of our successful entrepreneurs said that after every deal she has a debriefing session with her client, analyzing what has gone well and what hasn't, and focusing specifically on what the client has liked about both the results of the transaction and their relationship, as well as what he or she would like to change.

The luxury of choice

As her business grows, the entrepreneur can sometimes afford to be selective about clients or customers. At that stage, it is important to pay attention to personalities. Some clients will not accept or act on her advice. Some clients will always complain. Some will continue to test her, looking for her limits. Some will sabotage their own deals, unconsciously setting themselves up for failure. Some exist on the edge of panic, seeing impending crises in every deal and demanding constant reassurance. Some are loyal and appreciative, but will never grow enough to compensate the businessperson for the time they demand. It may not be worth the extra time and aggravation required to deal with "difficult" customers or clients. Some of our women said they continued to take on clients with such problems, but built a "hassle factor" into their fees to make the trouble worthwhile. Deciding how to deal with these problems, how to allocate her time and resources once she's established and growing, and how to attract new business with greater economic potential are continuing challenges to the entrepreneur.

DO I REALLY WANT THIS?

At this point in assessing the magnitude of the commitment she faces in beginning to market herself and her new business, it's a good idea for the entrepreneurial candidate to step back and reconsider. Is owning her own business truly her goal? Will she find in the business the kind of financial, emotional, intellectual, and "achievement" rewards she needs? Once she takes the step, she must put on blinders toward the rest of her life. She can't be distracted by other demands and interests. If she is going to start the business, it must be a total commitment and she must be prepared to make all the emotional adjustments and sacrifices necessary to succeed. Once she has started, it's too late to make plans and decisions about how to handle her obligations to her spouse, her children, her parents, her friends, and her volunteer organizations. Does this work-work-work syndrome ever stop? Yes! As the entrepreneur gradually achieves success in her business, she can begin to delegate some of her responsibilities. The work commitment is in direct proportion to the rate at which the company is growing: a fast-growing company will demand more of her time than would a more gradually paced business. For entrepreneurs of either sex, the bottom line generally dictates the time that must be committed to the business.

In reviewing the challenges and the many hidden roadblocks to entrepreneurial and personal success, our women achieved a new awareness. They were particularly sobered by how much hinges on the entrepreneur herself, on her ability and on her total commitment. Perhaps the least comfortable concept was that of the entrepreneur continually selling herself — and making the client's or customer's interests come first — if she wants to make a success of her new venture.

PART FOUR

WOMEN IN PERSPECTIVE

Our group has covered a lot of ground in a few years. We've all grown, many of us have prospered, some of us have failed and started again. We've learned from one another and from our new capacity to appreciate women and their leadership abilities. And we've begun to put our own experiences and insights into a wider societal perspective.

THIRTEEN

The Changing Role of American Women

THE HISTORICAL PERSPECTIVE

It's important as we try to establish ourselves comfortably in our new role in "womantime" to have a clear perspective of where we've been and how far we've come. And to recognize that we are still in the early days of this wonderful new era.

It's interesting to take a look at the evolution of American women in the workplace. During the American Revolutionary War, while the men were fighting, women took over the management of family farms and local businesses. The political leaders of our new country were able to function as such because their wives kept their families and businesses intact while the men were off winning our independence politically and in battle. Of course the women also continued to fulfill their roles as homemakers and nurturers of children. Almost 100 years later, during the American Civil War when so many of this country's men were killed, women (especially in the South) again came to the fore to maintain and feed their families until a new generation of male children grew up to take over family enterprises. During World War II, when the men went off to battle, the women became the dependable work force that kept our factories producing the goods essential to the war effort. "Rosie the Riveter" was the symbol of the American woman who showed the world her ability to perform what was traditionally "men's work."

The period following World War II saw many changes in this country. One of the most significant was that the women who had rallied to the workplace to fill the gap left by our fighting men didn't necessarily *want* to return to their old roles as homemakers. Many of them enjoyed working outside the home, and wanted to continue. Further, the old stereotypes of what was "appropriate" work for women had been seriously undermined. Coupled with this subtle change in attitude was a new social and economic situation in this country. In the period of postwar prosperity, there was a surge in the invention and production of consumer goods, many of them convenience items that reduced the burden of housekeeping: automatic washers and dryers, automatic dishwashers, wrinkle-free garments, frost-free refrigerators and home freezers, microwave ovens, and frozen packaged foods all added free time for women who worked as homemakers. For the first time, they had hours available to do something outside the home. Since these convenience items were also expensive, for many women the "opportunity" to enjoy free time was won when they earned money to pay for the tools that created it. A climate was created in which women not only *could* work outside the home, but often had to do so to be able to enjoy the quality of life they wanted for themselves and their families.[17]

In 1950, 34 percent of American women were employed outside the home. By 1975 that figure had increased to 46 percent. Today, 55 percent of American women are in paid employment, and 54 percent of women with children under three years of age are in the work force. Women constitute five out of every six workers in the service-producing sector of our economy. In 1985 they represented 58.8 percent of all workers in finance, insurance, and real estate, 89.9 percent of health service workers, and 44.6 percent of workers in communications and the media.[18]

As women have taken their place in the work force at various stages in our history, there have also been surges of political activity revolving around their needs and interests. But it wasn't until the early 1960s that women began to surface as an organized segment of our society. That was a time when many of our institutions were going through periods of great change and upheaval. It was also a time when the role of women began to change dramatically, and those changes gradually had an impact on our way of life. The role of women in leadership began to crystallize in the 1970s, when women truly became a separate, and distinctly influential, power group. During that exciting decade, many of us first began to generate a positive image of ourselves as persons in our own right.

The legacy of the ERA

Many women in the United States were deeply disappointed when we lost our fight for the Equal Rights Amendment. Despite this loss, in a real sense we won a great victory: as a power group, we developed a strong leadership identity and became highly visible. Since then, women have been making an increasingly strong impact on our country. Just consider, for example, the effectiveness of Mothers Against Drunk Drivers (MADD) in California. This group of women single-handedly, quietly, and within a very short time, had laws passed through the California legislature that levied severe penalties against drunk drivers. Those women, and many others organized today in strong and influential women's networks, are the indirect result of the unification and political awareness begun by the fight for the ERA. We now *know* we can make a difference, so we organize in order to do so.

Another legacy of the ERA is, ironically, summed up in the argument used by many of the men and women who opposed the concept of equal rights for women. They said that once women attained equal status, they would no longer have the luxury of being put on a pedestal and treated as women. Well, we may not yet have attained truly equal status, but what those critics threatened is already a reality for women, whether it has been widely recognized and acknowledged or not. For good or bad — and I happen to think for good — female children can no longer be raised with the idea that they need not educate themselves for future careers because one day they will marry, raise a family, and be taken care of by their husbands. This myth ceased to be a reality even before the advocates of

ERA began urging society to make equal demands on women, along with guaranteeing them equal rights. Today, one of the largest poverty groups in our country is composed of divorced or widowed women who are single heads of households, many of them with children to raise, who are neither well provided for by former husbands nor capable of entering the work force at a living wage. A statistic quoted in *The New York Times Magazine* (October 26, 1986) suggests the magnitude of the problem for divorced women: "When a couple splits up, the man's standard of living goes up 42 percent while the woman's (and children's) drops 73 percent." Because they bought into the idea of marrying, staying at home, and "living happily ever after," these women are paying the price of being alone to make their way in society without adequate resources. They have lost the financial security they enjoyed as wives, and they haven't the skills or mental and emotional preparation to attain such security independently. They represent a huge social problem, still crying out for a solution. If there is one lesson we should have learned from the experience of this circumstantially created underclass, it is that young women, like young men, must be educated and trained to support themselves. They must be encouraged to achieve at the highest level of which they are capable, and to extend that achievement into business or professional life.

Even when she opts to stay at home to raise her children, a woman should be prepared to the very best of her ability to go back into the work force when her children grow up and become independent. She should always feel that she has options, either to go back to work and become financially independent or to remain at home, and she should feel confident of her productivity in either role. Women who do not seek financial independence often find a creative outlet in volunteer work or politics. The key is preparedness, which gives a woman the security of selecting among several options.

The lesson of networking

Through organizing politically, women have come to recognize the strength we gain from one another. Out of this realization has come the kind of informal networking that has been of such importance to the women in our group (and in hundreds or even thousands of other women's networks around the country). We have learned to appreciate and respect one another as individuals, as professionals, and as leaders. By seeing our own accomplishments through the eyes of other women, we also have come to appreciate and respect ourselves for what we are and what we can do. And we're acting on these new and stimulating perceptions.

After more than five years of fulfilling association with other "Women in Management," those who have been part of our group have learned a great deal. We recognize who we are, and we accept that we are leaders and role models for the women who will follow us. We know that one of the secrets to success is self-confidence, and we know that in order to grow in self-confidence we must learn to sell ourselves convincingly to others. We know if we have what it takes to be entrepreneurs, and what will be expected of us in terms of hard work and sacrifice. We know where to turn for financing, and we have learned how to use our existing contacts and develop new ones to help our businesses take off. We have a lot of ideas about what to do — and almost as many about what *not* to do — as we establish ourselves in business and in life.

We also have the gratification of knowing that there are others who care and who can offer support and understanding through the network we have developed, and that our network will continue to expand. We've gained a new appreciation of what a mentor can do for us, and we know a little bit about what we can give other women by becoming mentors ourselves.

I am very grateful for all that participation in our group has taught me, and especially grateful to the warm, caring, and sharing women who have helped me learn and understand. For them, and for the many women who will follow us up the leadership ladder, I want to offer in summarized form the credo I have developed as a result of my own experience, which is enriched by the experiences of all the women in our group. I call this credo "Ronya's Rules." Here they are, with thanks to those who have helped me formulate them.

RONYA'S RULES

1. *Understand the concepts of power and status*

Make them work for you and do not become a slave to them.
They should be used as tools, and they must not be abused.
Using power and status in the finest sense does not mean just
playing negative political games. It does mean being goal
directed and working toward common objectives to better
your organization.

2. *Have an enormous reservoir of patience*

It is imperative for a woman in a leadership position, particularly if she interacts principally with men, not to "blow her
cool." It really is possible to be firm and not lose your temper.
If you want to succeed, and to accomplish your goals, learn to
wait for an appropriate opportunity to make your point without showing irritation or frustration. Let others lose their
tempers. One thing I have learned is that it drives men up the
wall when they cannot make a woman blow her cool. The best
thing you can do is "kill them with kindness," especially when
they are most upset.

3. *Work very hard*

Women still have to work harder than men to get ahead. Consider this a blessing, a positive impetus. The biggest advantage
a woman has is her innate ability to juggle three or four different jobs at one time. Successful women are forced to be highly
efficient through desperate necessity. I hope we never lose
either our ability or our desire to preserve this culturally man-
dated talent for efficient time management!

4. *Don't throw your weight around*

The people who work for you, if you are a boss, deserve your
trust, respect, and open communication. They also need to be
rewarded. Give credit to subordinates and appreciate their
efforts. When a boss gives credit to a subordinate, it reflects
positively on the boss. A secretary is vital to a boss's success.
Be particularly kind and sensitive to the feelings of your secretary. A good secretary can be the nerve center of a smoothly
running organization. Always remember that an unwilling-

ness to relate to secretaries, or subordinates, or younger people in junior management positions is a clear indication of your own insecurity in your position.

5. *Help the younger women behind you*
Don't have the mistaken attitude, "I had it hard, now I'll make it hard for her." Help the young women behind you even if they surpass you. If they are competent and deserving, both of you become winners, and the biggest winners of all are the organization you serve and the community in which you live. A lot who are deserving will be passed by. Don't brood on it, just go on to something else. On the other hand, there will be many who will surge forward. Applaud them and boost them at every opportunity.

6. *Be tenacious*
Don't give in to discouragement and depression. Women leaders are still in the minority. Don't be angry and hostile when things are not fair. (I guarantee you, they *won't* always be fair.) There is a difference between being right and winning. Sometimes you will be right and not win. The posture for us as women leaders is not to be discouraged by losing, even when we know we're right.

7. *Ignore a lot and be very flexible*
It is inevitable that, as a woman in a management and leadership role, you will have some real bums to deal with. Do your job as well as you are able, and ignore them. Many times it will be necessary for you to change your focus. Your supervisors or peers may also need to change their directions. Being able to change course quickly and effectively may make the difference in your organization. In a company, being able to change quickly may well be the difference between success and failure. No matter what happens, do your best, work hard. Most of the time, this will pay off. As a leader nobody "promised you a rose garden," so don't expect one.

8. *Trust to luck*
Luck plays a great part in leadership. Luck, however, is not always an intangible. I like to say there are two kinds of luck:

luck that just happens, and the other kind that comes along when you are just watching, and you see it and grab it. Being in the right place at the right time is important, but it is also imperative to be aware of the opportunity that is there for you, and to have the courage, conviction, ability, and, most of all, the endurance to seize it and make it happen. To make luck happen takes hard work and dedication.

9. Don't take yourself too seriously
Pompous, officious women can be a real drag. Having a sense of humor is an absolute must for any leader. For a woman leader it is a special imperative. Because women leaders are still the "new kids on the block," it is important for them to make a habit of laughing. If they don't, they'll cry a lot, and crying is definitely counterproductive. A sense of humor will bring out the best in people around you, and that's what leadership is all about.

10. Believe in and trust your women's intuition
This is a special ability that has been honed by centuries of cultural adaptation. It is a real feminine tool and should be used intelligently to benefit everyone in an organization. As moral and ethical issues arise in your company, trust your instinct. Chances are your instinct will be right.

These rules may not contain all the secrets for a woman launching herself in business, but they'll certainly give her a head start.

A final word of thanks
As I hope this book demonstrates, I am a great admirer of the women who have given so generously of themselves during their participation in the Women in Management group. I hope that their experiences and advice, as reflected here, will be of value to other women who share their enthusiasm and their frustrations, and who are seeking their own innovative solutions to the new challenges offered in this exciting era of womantime.

[17]Ronya Kozmetsky, RGK Foundation, Austin, Texas, "The Role of Women Managers and Women Entrepreneurs in Today's American Society" (speech, 5th Annual Women & Work Conference, Arlington, Texas, May 12–13, 1988).

[18]Laura Lein, Teresa Sullivan, and Rhobia Taylor, "Women, Technology, and Employment: The Labor Force of the Future. Workplace 2000" (proceedings of a conference sponsored by the United States Department of Labor, Women's Bureau, the University of Texas at Austin, and the Texas Employment Commission, Austin, Texas, December 10, 1987).